When the Hurt Won't Go Away

When the Hurt Won't Go Away

Paul W. Powell

Though this book is designed for the reader's
personal enjoyment, it is also intended for group
study. A Leader's Guide with Victor Multiuse
Transparency Masters is available from your
local bookstore or from the publisher.

VICTOR

BOOKS a division of SP Publications, Inc.
WHEATON, ILLINOIS 60187

Offices also in
Whitby, Ontario, Canada
Amersham-on-the-Hill, Bucks, England

Recommended Dewey Decimal Classification: 223.1
Suggested Subject Heading: JOB

Library of Congress Catalog Card Number: 85-62721
ISBN: 0-89693-365-2

CONTENTS

ACKNOWLEDGMENTS

This book is possible only because of the help of many other people, most of them volunteers, who have been willing to give of themselves freely. I would be remiss if I did not, from the outset, acknowledge my appreciation of all of them.

Gloria Ortega, my dedicated and efficient secretary of eleven years, comes first. She typed and retyped the original manuscript while maintaining her usual pressing work load at the church office.

Then comes Gerrie Milburn, an English teacher who proofread the manuscript for spelling, punctuation, and grammatical errors.

Gerrie is herself a modern-day Job.

Five years ago she had a mastectomy. A year later her husband was killed in an automobile-train collision. A year after that she had additional surgery for a brain tumor. Twice she has suffered the humiliation of losing all her hair from chemotherapy treatments. Now doctors have given her only a few weeks to live.

Through all of this, like Job, Gerrie " . . . sinned not, nor charged God foolishly" (Job 1:22). Rather she has worked diligently and cheerfully and pressed me to do the same. She is a flesh and blood example of "How to live! How to die!"

Anita Anderson is next. She is a special friend who helped by retyping the manuscript in its final form during her summer vacation.

Finally, Mark Bockmon, a free-lance writer and the unofficial mayor of Mineola, Texas, took my work and added his touch to it, all as a ministry for the Lord.

To these four special friends and to my wonderful congregation I acknowledge my gratitude and my debt.

PAUL W. POWELL
Green Acres Baptist Church
1612 Leo Lynn
Tyler, Texas 75701

PREFACE

- A young mother learns she has terminal cancer.
- A bus taking a church group to a ski resort overturns, injuring many and leaving one young woman permanently paralyzed.
- A child crossing a street is struck by a car and killed.
- A Christian girl is abducted by two men. Though she shares Jesus with them and pleads for mercy, she is brutally raped, tortured, and murdered.
- A missionary is killed by the tribe he came to serve.
- A young father, working a second job as a convenience store clerk, is killed by a teenager on drugs who holds up the store.

True stories like these fill our daily newspapers. They pervade our coffee-time conversation. They are the substance of countless prayer requests. All around us, people are hurting. Good people. With anguish and tears, we look heavenward and one overriding question permeates our prayers: WHY?

HOW DO YOU COPE WHEN THE WORST THINGS HAPPEN TO THE BEST PEOPLE?

WHY HER?
WHY HIM?
WHY US?
WHY ME?

The answer is not always easy. Complex questions seldom have simple answers. But insights can be found by a study of the Scriptures. In this book, rather than studying many vignettes, we focus on one man's suffering, its causes, and how he and his friends reacted to it.

The man's name was Job. In his day he was the wealthiest, most respected man in his part of the world. He was a man of unimpeachable character. God himself attested to that. Then tragedy struck. In a series of unexplainable incidences that involved both natural calamity and human evil, Job lost almost everything he considered worthwhile in life—his children, his wealth, his health, and his reputation.

Holding on only to his integrity and a slender thread of faith, Job grappled with the same questions and emotions that have haunted sufferers of all ages. But nothing he heard or experienced satisfied him.

It was not until he met God in person, came to know Him other than by hearsay, that he found peace. Once he heard God, answers were not necessary. It is the same with us today.

From a study of this godly man's experiences and responses we can learn much about how to live and how to die. As we walk with Job from the mountaintop of success, through the valley of sorrow and suffering, and then back to the mountaintop again, Job can show us how to cope when the worst of things happen to the best of people.

If these pages help you in that way, then they will have accomplished their purpose. That is why they have been written, and it is with a prayer to that end they are offered.

FOREWORD

Job, perhaps the oldest book in the world, was written to help answer the oldest question in the world, "Why do the righteous suffer?"

In spite of the current deluge of "health-and-wealth theology," the fact of the matter is that Jesus promised His followers only three things in this life: they would be always in trouble, never alone, ever at peace. The Christian faith was never intended to be merely an absence of human suffering; it is, rather, comfort in the midst of the storm, God's working out His purposes, revealing His grace, blessing with His presence. We get sick, we get divorces, we lose our jobs, our kids go bad like everybody else's. But we don't have to blow our brains out or jump off tall buildings! We have a Saviour who has answers, help, a purpose, and a presence to reveal through it all.

In his marvelous book, *When the Hurt Won't Go Away*, Paul Powell has cut to the quick of the problem with uncanny insight. One of the classic arguments against Christianity, yea, against all systems of organized religious thought, is Why do the righteous suffer? The bottom line in Job is that he never really learns why, but comes to the maturity that says, "It really doesn't matter; I don't have to know. God is not accountable to me; I am accountable to Him. Therefore, "Though He slay me, yet will I trust Him." It is essentially the answer to which the writer of Ecclesiastes came when he sought to unscramble the inequities of life and resolved the whole issue with a simple, "Let us hear the conclusion of the whole matter; fear God and keep His commandments."

Your journey through these pages may well prove it to be the most incisive treatise you have ever studied as it was for me on this question of questions.

Paul Powell has done a great service to the Christian community with this masterful work. Happy reading!

JOHN R. BISAGNO, Pastor
First Baptist Church, Houston, Texas

Dedicated
to
Kay and Mittie Barron
who
lost their only son
but
did not lose faith
in
God's only Son

chapter 1
WHEN THE WORST THINGS HAPPEN TO THE BEST PEOPLE

Nothing so shakes our faith in the fairness of God as to see unjust, senseless suffering—a young mother who becomes an invalid, an innocent child stricken by disease, a man in the prime of life who dies from a massive heart attack. We wish we could believe in a just and fair world, but time and again we have seen the wrong people get sick, the wrong people be hurt, the wrong people die young.

"Why, God?" we ask. "Why?" How could a good God make a world like this, where so much of the suffering falls on those who least deserve it?

We have in the Old Testament man, Job, a person who goes through extreme personal agony and can give us some answers to these questions. The Book of Job is the oldest book in the Bible. It is fitting that it wrestles more earnestly with this question of suffering than any other book in history.

The Book of Job is a real live drama that begins like a fairy tale. Job is one of the wealthiest and most respected men in the East. He is surrounded by what are commonly regarded as unmistakable tokens of divine favor—a large family, immense herds of cattle, sheep, and camels, vigorous health, a good reputation, and great power. It looks as though every cloud in Job's sky has a silver lining.

But before his story progresses very far the dark clouds of sorrow and suffering begin gathering over Job's pleasant life. And before the storm is over Job will lose everything he values except his life and his faith. As tragedies keep striking, the silver lining of Job's life turns to brass and he is suddenly plunged into such depths of despair that he feels abandoned by God. Job's wife and his friends add to his misery by offering cheap, easy answers to his agonizing questions. Though they mean well, they do great harm.

In all of this Job's faith bends but it does not break. And in the end God vindicates Job's character by restoring to him more than he had originally lost.

The story ends as it began, with Job blessed and happy. But in between, Job grapples with life's most common and yet most distressing question: "Why do the worst of things happen to the best of people?" As we walk with Job through his wrenching pain, he teaches us how to live and how to die. These are things we all desperately need to know.

After being briefly introduced to Job's good life, the scene shifts from earth to heaven where Satan appears before God and accuses Job of having a shallow and superficial faith. What do you believe about Satan? The Bible pictures Satan as person, not just an evil influence. He is presented in Scripture as the enemy of both God and people. It is clear that Satan's purpose is to destroy Job's faith and thus to discredit God. Job is such a godly man with such a good reputation that if Satan can shake his faith in God the tremors will be felt everywhere Job is known. Because others are watching Job, his reaction will affect their faith also.

Have you come to realize that none of us lives in a spiritual vacuum? There is an evil one at work in our world who would delight to shatter our confidence in God to the point that we abandon Him. If Satan can get good people to become bitter and doubting, he not only destroys their faith but he also casts a shadow over the credibility of God in the minds of other people.

Satan begins by questioning the sincerity of Job's commitment to God and accuses Job of serving God only for what he can get out of Him. Satan claims that God has built a hedge of protection around Job so that no evil can touch him. Satan says that if that hedge is taken down and Job loses his blessings, he will also lose his religion.

This, of course, is not true, but the charge has been made and God will defend the character of this good man. So Satan is allowed to bring suffering and sorrow into Job's life to prove that his accusations are wrong.

No one except God really knows the quality of Job's faith until it is tested. So, with divine permission, Satan begins to test Job. First, all of Job's wealth is either stolen or destroyed by natural calamities. Then the house where his children have gathered is struck by a tornado and ten of them die violent deaths.

Suddenly Job finds himself as desolate and bereft as a human being can be. But in all of this, Job remains true to God. His faith stands up against Satan's first test.

Satan is not through, however. He never gives up easily on good people. So once more he appears before God and assaults Job's character. This time the devil says that if he can afflict Job's body the man will actually curse God. Again God "gambles" on Job's character and grants Satan permission to afflict him with pain. But he is forbidden to take Job's life. Job's body is then covered with sores that cause such excruciating pain that he sits in the soft ashes of the city dump and weeps in despair. His pain is made even more unbearable because he cannot understand why all of this is happening to him.

What a pathetic scene! Job, who was until recently one of the greatest men of the East, is now grieving and destitute. His wealth is gone, his children are dead, and his body is wracked with pain.

Depressed and distraught, Job wishes he could die. Furthermore, he wishes he had never been born. He is no longer sure even about eternity. He asks himself, "If a man die shall he live again?" (Job. 14:14) Feeling that God has deserted him, he cries out, "Oh, that I knew where I might find Him! That I might come even to His seat!" (23:3)

Sorrow and suffering can do that to you. They can so shake your faith that they cause you to question almost everything you once held sacred and true. Let me pause to remind you of two crucial truths you must not miss in Job's experience. The first truth is that Job's suffering is not caused by God but by Satan. God permits it but He doesn't cause it. There is a vast difference.

The second important fact is that Job never knows anything about the scenes in heaven. Throughout all of his suffering he is never told why it is happening. We are given the revelation from God so we know, but Job never does. He is left to struggle in the darkness of his sorrow and pain without ever being told why. If he had been told why, no real test of his faith would have taken place. Is it any wonder that Job feels deserted and alone without God? We are not the least surprised to hear him cry out to the Lord, "Why me, God? Why me?"

Have you ever felt that way? You may be feeling that way right now. You are hurting and you don't understand why. You see no light at the end of the tunnel. You may be saying, "O God, if You are a loving God, why are You letting this happen to me? Why did You take my husband? Why do I have cancer? Why are my children unsaved? Why did my wife divorce me?"

In the remainder of the Book of Job several efforts are made to help Job understand his suffering. Though God is silent about why this is all happening to Job, others aren't. His wife, three of his closest friends, and finally a young intellectual all come to him. All of them except his wife try to explain his misfortunes. Though these people are all very sincere, they are sincerely wrong and their answers are thoroughly unacceptable.

Finally God comes to Job's rescue. He does not explain Job's suffering but He reveals Himself to Job in such a dramatic way that when Job hears God, he is satisfied. He can live without an answer because he now has an awareness of God.

In reading about Job's experience we have a chance to struggle with him as he asks the questions we have often asked about suffering and sorrow. And we have an opportunity to learn some of life's greatest lessons about how to live and how to die.

DOES GOD PLAY FAIR?

Job's wife is the first to offer counsel to him. She proposes a simple solution to Job's problem: "Curse God and die" (2:9). Her conclusion is: "Job, you have been true to God, but God has not been true to you. You can't change what's happened to us but at least you can have the satisfaction of having the last word."

Job's wife believes that God is not fair and that people are helpless pawns at the mercy of His whims. All of her life she has accepted the good things that have come to her without any questions. But now that trouble has come, she is bitter and cynical and ready to fling away her faith.

Job is wiser than his wife. Though there is much he does not know, he at least knows that this is not the right solution to his problem. Maybe he has known God longer; he certainly knows God better than his wife does. God is not unfair. God does not play the game of life dishonestly.

Job has enjoyed the good life with gratefulness. Now he accepts each new shock wave of loss with quietness and courage. At first there is no word of bitterness or despair on his lips (2:10).

How wise and how consistent Job is. He is mature enough to know that if evil causes us to doubt God, then good should cause us to affirm God. We cannot concentrate only on one aspect of life and ignore the other. If evil needs an explanation, so does good. If trouble shakes your faith in God, then the good of life ought to steady it. If suffering tempts you to curse God, then blessings ought to lead you to praise God.

If we expect God to be consistent, we are obligated to be consistent ourselves. Surely the God of heaven who sent His Son to die for our sins is righteous in His dealings with us.

Do you remember the story (Gen. 18) of God's appearing to Abraham and Sarah to reconfirm His promise to them? On that occasion God also shared with Abraham that He was planning to destroy Sodom and Gomorrah because of their grievous sin. But Abraham, knowing that his nephew Lot and his family resided there, pleaded with God to stay His judgment even if only ten righteous people could be found in those cities. Abraham's plea was, "Shall not the Judge of the earth do right?" (18:25)

Have you ever doubted the integrity of God? Have you ever wondered if God is fair and true? Whatever your difficulty or burden might be, never forget the testimony of Scripture and history is that the problem lies not with God. He is gracious; He is righteous; He is always fair. The problem lies with us.

THE LAW OF THE HARVEST

Job's second visit is from three of his friends. We can have no greater blessing in times of trouble than true friends. Nothing can be more comforting to us than the help of wise, considerate friends—but nothing can be more devastating than the counsel of misguided ones.

Eliphaz, Bildad, and Zophar are true friends. Job has been numbed into silence by his troubles. Nearly everyone has this initial reaction to the trauma of severe loss. There is so much within us that doesn't want to accept the actuality of what has happened. So Job's friends sit with him for seven days and seven nights without saying a word. They realize that Job's agony of body and soul is such that anything they can say would be of no comfort. So they wisely keep quiet.

The ministry of silence is often of more value than the ministry of words. Sitting quietly with a suffering friend is often the best comfort we can give.

But after a week, the awful reality of what has occurred is really torturing Job and he starts to complain about his condition. At this point everything looks utterly hopeless to him. He bemoans the day he was born and makes it clear that if he could die immediately it would suit him just fine (chap. 3). Job sees no future left for him. When Job starts to complain, his friends feel compelled to offer an explanation as to why he is suffering.

All three of them mouth the most common explanation for suffering in their day. Though they all argue from different perspectives, they come eventually to the same conclusion. It can be summed up in the words of Eliphaz, "Remember, I pray thee, whoever perished being innocent? Or where were the righteous cut off? Even as I have seen, they that plow iniquity, and sow wickedness, reap the same" (4:7-8). These friends point to the law of harvest—we reap what we have sown. Their explanation: Job is suffering because of his sins. They firmly believe that the judgment of God has come upon him.

They figure that since Job is reaping so much trouble he must have sown iniquity. Since Job's life is outwardly such a deeply religious one, they surmise that he must have some horrible secret sins in his life, so they urge him to confess them.

Sound familiar? This was not only the most common explanation for suffering in Job's day. It is also the most common explanation of suffering in our day. Not long ago I visited with an eighty-one-year-old woman in a nursing home. She was suffering not only from a broken hip but also from this great misconception. All of her life she had been active and independent. Now because of a fall she had been placed in a nursing home. An infection in her hip had further complicated her chances of recovery. Amid her pain and her tears, she said, "I have prayed to die. I don't know why the good Lord doesn't take me on home. I know I haven't been perfect, but I don't know what I've done to deserve this. I can't see why I have to suffer this pain."

See how common this idea is? Almost everyone seems to look on suffering as a punishment from God.

The God of the Bible is a God of justice. We do reap what we have sown (Gal. 6:7). Judgment Day is coming. We must not expect to escape the consequences of our actions forever. If we do, we are destined for disillusionment. We all know of good people who suffer and evil people who prosper. There is apparently little justice here and now. God never promised complete justice in this life, so it should not be expected until the end of time.

These three friends of Job mean well, but the way they proceed to deal with his crisis makes an already bad situation worse. They do a very common thing—they try to intellectualize life. Job is trying desperately just to cope, to muster up enough strength to endure one more hour of pain and adjust to the new set of circumstances that are so radically different from his past. What he needs at this time is understanding and compassion and a sense of hope, but that is not what his friends are interested in offering him. Instead they offer "an explanation to life." To further complicate matters, in Job's case their explanation is wrong.

It angers Job that his friends are so insensitive to what he really needs at the moment. Job is not a perfect man and he knows it. However, his sin is not serious enough to merit all that is befalling him and he knows that too. You don't treat dandruff with a guillotine. Job's present judgment in no way matched his sins. It is too severe for what he has done. So Job vehemently and consistently denies their accusations.

As the discussion goes on Job gets madder and madder, first at his friends and their neat oversimplifications and finally at God for allowing all of his trouble to happen. Job finds himself shouting that there is a mystery to both good and evil that no mechanistic equation can explain.

Job's friends have come to him with the best of intentions but instead they keep hurting him deeply. I'm not sure Job would have ever started down the path of anger and complaining if it had not been for them. Their problem is that they give easy answers to life's most complex problem.

If we are wise in trying to help our hurting friends, we will not make the same mistake. We will take more of a position of humility before their sorrow and pain, realizing that there is no one answer and often no answer at all that we can be sure of.

LEARNING TO LEAN

Then comes Elihu (chaps. 32—37). Elihu is a young intellectual who has listened to Job debate with his three friends until all four men have exhausted all of their arguments. When they are through, Elihu can keep silent no longer.

Elihu was like some intellectuals who deal only in secondhand experiences. What they know they have either read in books or have heard from somebody else. They usually deal in theory and not in experience. That analysis fits Elihu perfectly.

Elihu emphasizes the creative value of suffering. He argues that Job's suffering is an act of discipline from God to teach him lessons he needs to learn.

This explanation of suffering is often spoken of in the Bible.

As a psalmist writes, "Before I was afflicted I went astray; but now have I kept Thy Word" (Ps. 119:67). And, "It is good for me that I have been afflicted, that I might learn Thy statutes" (Ps. 119:71).

There is much truth in Elihu's words. God wants to make us more like His Son Jesus and to accomplish that, He uses all kinds of experiences—even those He does not cause (Rom. 8:28).

Some testings are even designed by God to accomplish His gracious purposes in our lives. The Apostle Paul's life is a good example of this. He relates that he suffered some physical ailment which he called "a thorn in the flesh" that caused him a great deal of pain (2 Cor. 12:7-9). When he asked God to relieve him of it, God's answer was no.

Paul perceived that the thorn was given him, not for punishment, but for protection. His physical weakness guarded him against pride, as he put it, to keep him from being too elated by "the abundance of the revelations" (NKJV) God gave him. Seeing that was so, he could accept it as a wise provision on the part of the Lord. He even embraced his continuing disability as a kind of privilege. God uses chronic pain and weakness, along with other sorts of afflictions, as His chisel for sculpturing our souls. Felt weakness deepens dependence on Christ for strength each day. The weaker we feel, the harder we lean. And the harder we lean, the stronger we grow spiritually, even while our bodies waste away.

But suffering is not always the result of sin. Difficulties are not always because of personal failure. Not all suffering is sent to discipline or to teach us. Some is, but not all. This is Elihu's mistake.

KNOWING GOD

The approach God takes with Job is the direct opposite of what his four friends have tried. God makes no attempt to "explain" the process of tragedy to Job for two obvious reasons. First, Job is in no position to understand ultimate answers even if they are given him. They belong to the realm of the infinite and are beyond him. Second, answers are not what Job needs most at this moment. If God were to give him all of the facts he would still be in pain and have to deal with the empty chairs and the poverty.

What Job needs is "grace sufficient," not to know it all but to bear it all. So, God doesn't give Job an answer. He gives Job Himself as the answer. He takes Job on a mental tour of the universe and bids him observe the wonder and the mystery of the world in which he is placed. God points out the constellations in the heavens and asks Job, "Where were you when I put the stars in their orbit? Where were you when I placed the planets in the heavens?" (38:4-7) In all of this, Job gains a new appreciation for God's power, His sovereignty over all things.

Then God takes him on a tour of the animal kingdom. He points out the features of several animals and asks Job, "Can you explain why I made these animals the way I did?" (38:39—39:30; 40:15—41:34)

Job does not have an answer for God, but he learns something about God that he did not know before. In being asked question after question, Job becomes aware of how little he knows and how wise God is. He realizes how presumptuous he has been in questioning anything that God has done.

Awed to silence, Job is driven to his knees in humility at the power and the wisdom of God. The frail creature bows before the mighty Creator and declares, "I have heard of Thee by the hearing of the ear, but now mine eye seeth Thee" (42:5).

I repeat—God does not give Job an answer; that would not be enough. He gives Job Himself as the answer—His companionship, His courage, His hope. And that *is* enough.

Job is now able to face his suffering without knowing why all of it has happened. This is the great message of Job: if we know

God, we do not have to know why. In our suffering what we need most is not an explanation from God, but an experience with God. That alone is sufficient.

Job endures his trials and God blesses him in his old age with many rewards. There is a happy ending to the story as God restores to Job his health and his wealth, and gives him ten loving children.

Why do the godly suffer? It is not because God is unfair. He does not shoot dice with the lives of His children. It is not always because there is sin in our lives and He is punishing us for it. And it is not always because God is trying to teach us what we won't learn otherwise. In fact, in all probability we will never know in this life why we are suffering.

This may be hard to accept. We have inquiring minds. We want answers. But that's the way it is and if we are wise we will come to the place of accepting the infinite wisdom of God thankfully. That's the best way to live—and to die.

chapter 2

I NEVER PROMISED YOU
A ROSE GARDEN

Not long ago in a time of great distress over one of our children, my wife said to me, "I just don't understand why the Lord let this happen to us." I had been studying the Book of Job at the time and one of the lessons of life that I had learned from it was that God builds no walls of protection around His children to shield them from any of life's hurts.

When Satan appears before God in heaven, he accuses God of just that. He insinuates that the only reason Job is serving God is for what he can get out of Him. Satan accuses God of putting a hedge around Job and his house to protect him from tragedy, loss, and harm so that everything Job does prospers. For at first Job has health, a wonderful family, a good reputation, and abundant wealth. Who wouldn't serve God under those conditions?

But, suggests Satan, if these things are taken away, if he can just afflict Job, it will be a different story. Job will then turn from God. Satan is sure that a few trials will reveal that Job's faith is shallow and superficial.

The Lord knows better. He knows that Job's faith is genuine

and sincere. Because God has such great confidence in the quality of Job's faith and to prove Satan's accusation wrong, He allows Satan to bring on Job the severest kinds of trials that a man could ever experience.

So, I said to my wife, "The Lord never promised to build a protective wall around any of us just because we are His children. And the fact that I am a minister and that we are trying to serve the Lord in no way guarantees that we are exempt from any of the problems of life. Satan is still at work seeking to destroy people's faith and we are as vulnerable as Job was."

This is a truth that we all need to understand. No one is exempt from any of life's trials so far as I know. Even if you are a faithful Christian and a concerned human being, trying your best to live right and help others, this will not keep the storms of life from coming to you. Christians get cancer. Christians suffer heart attacks. Christians have automobile accidents. And Christians go broke in business just like other people.

NO EXEMPTIONS

If ever a man should be exempt from trouble because of his good life, it is Job. He is one of the most godly, upright, and religious men ever to live. God calls Job "My servant" and says that there is "none like him in the earth" (2:3). Job is one of a kind. He is the best of the good men. The Lord attests to his character by saying that Job is spiritually mature, walks the straight and narrow path of life, reverences God, and turns away from evil (1:1). What a man! Yet despite such a sterling character Job is suffering as few people have ever suffered before or after his time.

If there were a candidate for exemption from trials in the New Testament, it would have been the Apostle Paul. If goodness, devotion, and heroism would exempt a person from dark hours, the Apostle Paul would have qualified. He gave himself with unflagging devotion to the cause of Christ. Yet his life was filled with so many storms that it seems he had to face emergency situations almost daily.

Paul tells about some of the mind-boggling, teeth-rattling, gut-wrenching experiences he faced as a missionary (2 Cor. 11:24-28). He was whipped at least five times with thirty-nine lashes on each occasion. He was beaten with sticks three other times. He was stoned at Lystra and left for dead; he suffered shipwreck on three occasions and as a result of one of them he was in the open seas for a day and a night.

In his many journeys he faced constant danger from the water, robbers who operated without restraint, and opposition from his own countrymen as well as from the heathen. Whether Paul was in the city or in the wilderness, on the seas or on the land, it was all the same. There were times when he was hungry, thirsty, and cold, without adequate clothing.

And if that were not enough, he carried on his missionary work while suffering constant and excruciating pain. He tells about this pain when he says, "There was given to me a thorn in the flesh, the messenger of Satan to buffet me" (2 Cor. 12:7).

The word *thorn* suggests the nature of his affliction. It was intensely painful. The word *flesh* locates it. This was not some person or a group of persons who troubled Paul. It was his flesh; it was a physical affliction. Guesses as to what this thorn was range from epilepsy to migraine headaches, and from malaria and the fever that accompanies it, to inflamed eyes (see Gal. 4:13-15). But nobody can be sure of what it was. We only know that it was an intensely painful physical affliction that he suffered.

The word *buffet* (2 Cor. 12:7) tells the effect this had on him. The word means "to strike" or "to rap" with the fist. This same word was used to describe what the soldiers did to Jesus at His trial before Pilate. They poked Him, punched Him, struck Him with their fists. Paul tells us that his painful physical affliction kept him beaten down. It was painful, crippling, frustrating, and humiliating.

In Paul's case prayer didn't help. He prayed for healing on at least three different occasions, but the healing did not come. Instead God's answer came back, "No, it is for your good that this has come. So, your affliction will continue but I will give you the grace to endure it, to cope with it, to stand up to it" (2 Cor. 12:8-9, author's paraphrase).

SHOULD WE PRAY FOR THE SICK?

Our prayers for deliverance and healing may not always be answered either. We need to remember that, lest we pray for healing and then lose confidence in God if our prayer is not answered.

There has come a revival of interest in healing in our churches today. It is much needed and long overdue. However, it is susceptible to much misunderstanding and abuse. Some of the new interest comes from God; much of it does not. A part of it comes from the fact that we are dazzled by the marvels of modern medicine. So many wonder drugs and new means of treatment have come about that we dream of abolishing ill health entirely in the here and now.

At the same time we are absorbed in pursuing bodily health through dieting and exercise and health foods. We are preoccupied with physical health, to which we feel we have a right. We are chasing a dream, a dream of never having to be ill. And there can be much worldliness in this preoccupation.

We are in danger of placing more emphasis on the body than on the soul. The worst diseases are those of the spirit: pride, conceit, arrogance, bitterness, and *self*-confidence are far worse and damage us far more than any malfunction of our bodies. Remember that John prayed for Gaius that he would prosper and be in health even as his soul prospered (3 John 2). Soul health should also be our first concern.

Don't get me wrong. I believe in and support good health practices. I try to keep my weight under control. I try to exercise adequately, eat correctly, and get an appropriate amount of rest. The body is the temple of the Holy Spirit and we ought to take care of it.

But even back in New Testament times Christian leaders such as Paul, who could not be accused of lacking faith, found that health and healing were never universal. We know from Acts that the Apostle Paul was sometimes Christ's agent in miraculous healing, and that he was himself once miraculously healed of a snake bite (Acts 28:3-6). Yet he advised Timothy, "Use a little wine for the sake of your stomach and your frequent ailments" (1 Tim. 5:23, NASB). In Timothy's case the infirmities were frequent, and he knew nothing of being kept in perfect health. So Paul instructed him to take a little wine for medicinal purposes.

Paul also informed Timothy that he had left Trophimus "sick" at Miletus (2 Tim. 4:20). And he told the Philippians how their messenger Epaphroditus was so sick that he was "nigh unto death" for the work of Christ (Phil. 2:27). The word *nigh* literally means "next-door neighbor to." Epaphroditus was so close to death that he was right next to it, within speaking distance. Perhaps Epaphroditus had worn himself out in God's service. You can do that in any kind of work—even Christian work.

How it grieved Paul to think of the prospects of losing Epaphroditus. Plainly, had Paul or anyone else sought power to heal these cases miraculously, Epaphroditus would have been disappointed. For as I have already pointed out, Paul himself lived with "a thorn in the flesh" that went unhealed.

Like Job and Paul, we too may suffer severe afflictions. And we may pray for healing with genuine faith, but the answer may be "no" or "not yet." We need to remember that. If we don't, when we suffer or when sorrow comes we will question the goodness and the justice of God and maybe even His existence. And when we pray for healing and it does not come we may question the efficacy of prayer.

"Well, then," you may ask, "should we even pray for the sick at all?" Yes, by all means. We not only should pray for the sick; we are commanded to do so. God is always able to deliver us from whatever besets us—but we need to realize that doing so may not be His plan.

Jesus healed abundantly in the days of His flesh and His power is still as great as it was then. However, we must remember that the healings He performed when He was on the earth had special significance. Besides being works of mercy, they were signs of His messianic identity (Isa. 35:5-6). And though He healed many, He did not want to be known as a miracle-worker.

No suffering Christian should fail to seek healing from God. But we cannot demand healing. God has not promised to heal every ailing Christian. Some He heals; others, like Paul and Timothy and Trophimus, He refuses for His own inscrutable reasons. A biblical Christian is willing to accept God's answer, whether it is yes or no. If he is healed, he gives God the glory. If he isn't, it doesn't shake his faith.

Besides, the very word *miracle* suggests that it is something unusual. If it happened all the time, then it would not be miraculous. It is only occasionally that God chooses to interrupt His laws that govern the universe and work a miracle.

A NO-ROSE-GARDEN LIFE
I have said all of this to say that God never promised us rose gardens. He offers us no trouble-free existence; He does not promise us lives of continuous joy, full of success, prosperity,

and good health. If by chance you are blessed with such a life now, you had better enjoy it today. Your life has no wall around it and before tomorrow Satan may well invade it and ravish it as he did in the case of Job.

God not only promises us no exemptions from troubles; most often He offers us no explanations for the sufferings of life. We may cry out to God "Why?" but usually no answer is forthcoming. The very silence of God sometimes causes us to feel that He rules the world with His hands off and His mouth shut.

If God grants us no exemptions and if He gives us no explanations, what should our expectations be? How does God help us? We need to know. One reason that so many people are easily disappointed and quickly disillusioned with Christian faith in times of trouble is that they have unreasonable and false expectations.

In his little book, *A Grief Observed,* C.S. Lewis tells about the death of his wife. He begins by openly acknowledging that at first he was keenly disappointed at what his Christian faith had meant to him in that experience. By the end of the book, however, in his usual perceptive way, he locates the problem as one of expectation more than experience. He realizes that he had taken into the valley certain notions of what ought to happen, and that, when those specific things did not happen, his disappointment almost blinded him to the things that were occurring. A realization of how God helps us is of crucial importance in saving us from false expectations.

GRACE SUFFICIENT

How does God help us? I can answer you in just one word— grace. When Paul asked for the removal of his thorn in the flesh, the answer came back, "My grace is sufficient for thee." God promised Paul that he would enable him to live with the experience. Grace is divine assistance. It is divine strength and supply. Though Paul's request was not granted, he received a far better answer.

The promise is that whatever suffering may come to us in the will of God can be met by the grace of God. God's provision is sure. He never allows heavier burdens on us than we can bear, for He is always present to share our burdens. If we depend on Him, God either lightens our loads or strengthens our backs to meet all of the experiences of life. He will enable us to bear the unbearable, to face the impossible, to get through. I can, no matter what the circumstances, always count on Him. I have learned that whenever crises overpower my waning strength, God reinforces. He stands ready to help.

Are you in the grip of pain and suffering? Then draw upon God's ready resources. He will strengthen. He will sustain. His grace is more than sufficient for every trial.

SAVED IN—NOT FROM

Though God does not exempt us from suffering and He does not explain to us why our suffering comes, He does enter into our experiences with us and helps us through them. God doesn't save us *from* trouble; He saves us *in* trouble.

God didn't save Daniel *from* the lions' den; He saved Daniel *in* the lions' den. He shut the mouths of the lions and kept them from devouring Daniel (Dan. 6).

God did not save the three Hebrew children *from* the fiery furnace; He saved them *in* the fiery furnace. He entered into the furnace with them and He became their shield to keep the fire from consuming them (Dan. 3).

And God did not route David around the valley of the shadow of death; He became David's Shepherd and walked with him through it (1 Sam. 18—29).

In the same way God does not save us from sorrow and suffering. But He loves us and enters into life's experiences to help us and to sustain us. Paul declares this when he asks, "Who shall separate us from the love of Christ?" (Rom. 8:35) Then he calls forth a list of life's most severe trials: tribulation, distress, persecution, famine, nakedness, peril, and the sword. Paul knew the reality of most of these things from personal experience and he knew that they could never separate us from the love of God. True, they can separate us from wealth and health. They can separate us from family and our friends. They can separate us from comfort and ease, but they can never separate us from the love of God. Instead, these experiences give opportunities for God's love in Christ to demonstrate its power and to give us victory over them.

So Paul declares that "in all these things we are more than conquerors through Him that loved us" (8:37).

NO SEPARATION
So there is nothing, Paul writes, that can ever separate us from the eternal and inexhaustible love of God. There is nothing in experience—"neither death nor life"; there is nothing in the heavens—neither "angels nor principalities nor powers"; there is nothing in time—neither "things present nor things to come"; there is nothing in space—neither "height nor depth"; and there is nothing on the earth—"nor any other creature" (8:38-39). Since there is nothing in experience, nothing in heaven, nothing in time, nothing in space, and nothing on earth that can separate us from the love of God, then nothing, absolutely nothing, will ever be able to do so.

Think of every terrifying thing that life can produce. None of these can ever separate us from the love of God. Because God loves us He enters into the sufferings and sorrows of life with us and makes us more than adequate for them through Christ.

Isaiah expressed this same promise when he wrote, "When thou passest through the waters, I will be with thee; and through rivers, they shall not overflow thee; when thou walkest through the fire, thou shalt not be burned; neither shall the flame kindle upon thee. . . . Fear not, for I am with thee" (Isa. 43:2, 5). God doesn't promise to keep our feet dry. He promises to keep us from drowning. He doesn't promise to keep us from being singed; He promises to keep us from being consumed. If we only have faith to believe that God will get us out, it isn't much faith. Usually God doesn't get us out—He gets us through.

The words of this poem by Annie Johnson Flint express this promise so well:

> *God hath not promised*
> *Skies always blue,*
> *Flower-strewn pathways*
> *All our lives through;*
> *God hath not promised*
> *Sun without rain,*
> *Joy without sorrow,*
> *Peace without pain.*
>
> *But God hath promised*
> *Strength for the day,*
> *Rest for the labor,*
> *Light for the way,*
> *Grace for the trials,*
> *Help from above,*
> *Unfailing sympathy,*
> *Undying love.*

In His famous Sermon on the Mount, Jesus related a story about two houses, one built on rock and the other built on sand (Matt. 7:24-27). The rains descended and the storms came and the wind blew on both houses. The house that was built on the sand fell. But the one that was built on the rock stood. The same rains and the same storms and the same winds hit both houses. The difference was not in the storms but in the buildings' foundations. What we need then is to build our lives on Christ, the solid Rock, so we can endure whatever storms come to us.

But because you build on the Rock doesn't mean that the storms of life won't come. It means that your house won't crumble when they do. I bear witness from my own experience to the sufficiency of God's grace—His saving grace and His sustaining grace. So build your life on Him, and when the storms come you will endure.

When Oliver Cromwell lay dying, it was a stormy night. The wind howled and shook the house until it seemed as if it would fall. After a while great, old rugged Cromwell said to the loved ones about him: "Read to me from Paul's letter to the Philippians. Read that to me." They read to him and when they read that great verse, "I can do all things through Christ who strengtheneth me," he said: "Stop just there. That was the word that saved me. When my son, Oliver, died, that was the word that saved me. When my heart was broken, that was the word that saved me. When sorrow swept down on our home as a black vulture, that was the word that saved me. When in one short hour all my sun was hid in midnight darkness, that was the word that saved me—'I can do all things through Christ who strengtheneth me.' "

And so, my friends, you can go to Christ and I can go, and ought to go, when trouble comes, no matter what form it assumes, no matter what guise or dress it wears. You can go to Him, and say: "Here am I, Lord. Put Thy hand on me. Put Thy Spirit in me. Make me to know that Thy promises are for me, and give me the sense of Thy grace, so that I shall be upborne, and shall not be afraid." And He will sustain you and give you the help you need.

If you have been going through some storms, I hope that by

the time you have finished reading this chapter you have found some peace with your pain and with God's silence. And if your confidence in prayer has been shaken, I hope that you will start praying again. God does not always give us our request, but He always gives us Himself! And that makes us sufficient. Knowing this can help us to live and to die victoriously.

chapter **3**

WHEN LIFE HANDS
YOU A LEMON

One of the most challenging statements in all of the Bible was made by Job when he asked, "Shall we indeed accept good from God and shall we not accept adversity?" (Job 2:10, NKJV)

Amen, Job! It is not right to take the good of life for granted and then complain about adversity.

This statement constitutes Job's reply to his wife's suggestion about how he should respond to his troubles. Job was a good and godly man and did not deserve what was happening to him. If anyone should know that about a man, it would be his wife. Job had served God devotedly before his trials, and during the beginning of them he maintained his pure and simple faith. But this was more than Mrs. Job could take. She just couldn't understand it and she wouldn't accept it. So she suggested that Job "curse God and die" (2:9).

Many people respond to trouble as Job's wife did. They go through life standing at the complaint counter. They feel that God owes them an easy life and that He is unjust if everything is not perfect. So, when trouble comes, they respond to it by becoming angry, bitter, and complaining against God.

Arthur J. Gossip, in a sermon that he preached just five days after his wife suddenly died, said, "I do not understand this life of ours. But still less can I comprehend how people in trouble and loss and bereavement can fling away peevishly from the Christian faith. In God's name, fling to what? Have we not lost enough without losing that too?"

We wonder, isn't there a better way to respond to trouble than this? Have we no better choice than to curse God and die?

Yes, there is a better way. It is Job's way. Job realized that life is a mixture. It is made up of good and of evil, of both the bitter and the sweet. Both of them splash against our lives indiscriminately.

Job knew that all sunshine and no rain makes a desert—that we cannot have mountaintops without valleys.

Job had accepted the good of life with a grateful spirit. Now he would try to endure the bad of life with a gracious spirit. He would take his losses with quietness and courage. There would be no bitterness in him. In this response Job teaches us much about how to live and how to die.

When Glenn Cunningham was a boy of eight, he and his brother attempted to start a fire to heat their school building. A violent kerosene explosion followed and Glenn's leg was so badly burned that the doctors proposed amputation. But his mother would not hear of it.

After six long months in the hospital, a series of extensive skin grafts, and endless hours of massaging by his mother's loving hands, Glenn began to walk and then to run to strengthen his crippled legs. He ran and he ran and he ran, until at age twenty-five he ran straight into a world record for the fastest mile—a record he was to hold for years.

The world applauded Cunningham's courage no less than his skill, for he had provided a thrilling illustration of the truth: "The world breaks everyone, but afterward many are strong in the broken places."

Indeed, sooner or later we are all broken. Defeat, disappointment, sorrow, and tragedy are the common lot of all people.

"Man," the Bible says, "is born to trouble as surely as sparks fly upward" (Job 5:7, NIV). Trouble is not a gate-crasher in the arena of our lives; it has a reserved seat there. Heartache has a passkey to every home in the land.

But, where trouble and suffering are concerned, you and I, like young Glenn, have the power not only to confront and endure them; we can use them constructively and creatively.

Life is like a grindstone. Whether we are ground down or polished up by it depends on what we are made of and how we respond to it. Troubles make some people better and others bitter. In their presence some people grow wings and others grab for crutches. Some become mellow, gentle, and soft. Others sink into self-pity, despair, or bitterness. More and more I realize that it is not what happens *to* us, but what happens *in* us that ultimately matters. We seldom have much control over what happens to us—but we always determine how it affects us. And it is our response to life that makes the difference.

George Buttrick once observed that "the same sun that hardens the clay melts the wax." Why is this, do you suppose, that an identical cause produces opposite effects? The answer lies in the response of the substance to the cause. In fact, reaction is just as important as initial action in the equation of events. This is particularly true when you are talking about human beings. We are different from all the rest of creation in that we have been given the gift of freedom. After all, the clay and the wax have no choice about how they react to the sun, but this is not the case with human beings. We are always free to determine what responses we will make to our given experiences.

Victor Frankl, in his book *Man's Search for Meaning*, describes the reaction of two brothers with the same heredity, the same environment, who exist in the same concentration camp under the Nazis. One became a saint and the other became like a swine. Frankl tells us the reason why. He said, "Each man has within him the power to choose how he will react to any given situation."

In fact, Frankl calls this "the last of the human freedoms." Everything else in life can be taken away from us—and perhaps life itself—but we are still free to determine how we will respond even to that.

We can choose to be like the clay and respond to the heat of life by letting it harden us and dry us out and make us bitter, or we can choose to be like wax and let what happens melt us and shape us into new patterns. Right here lies one of the central challenges of life. Often we humans are not free to determine what will happen to us, but we are free to determine what happens in us—how we will respond to these circumstances. One of the magnificent things about Job is that he refused to let his troubles make him become bitter, cynical, and calloused toward God.

THE ACID OF BITTERNESS

We have all seen people make what I call a "clay" response to circumstances; that is, they let some harsh misfortune turn them to bitterness and they foreclose on any meaningful future they might have had.

I have seen firsthand how the acid of bitterness can corrode a human spirit. And it is frightening to behold. I have run head-on into people—sometimes from prominent families, often well-educated, and frequently very talented—who live totally useless and withdrawn lives. Why? Because of one or more experiences of heartbreak that wounded them.

The sobering truth is that this sort of thing can happen to any one of us. After all, this life of ours is not a rose garden. If we live long enough, we will all experience tragedy and become "persons of sorrow, acquainted with grief." And if we choose, we can make a "clay" response to all of this and wind up as bitter and as hard as Job's wife.

TURNING LEMONS INTO LEMONADE

Fortunately, however, this is not the only option open to us. There is also a "wax" response; that is, allowing the circumstances to melt us and shape us in new ways.

I have also met people of this heroic stripe, who simply refuse to be overcome by the things that happen to them. In each case they turn out to be persons of flexibility and ingenuity and hope. They know how to respond "to a shipwreck of dreams"; that is, instead of going down in despair or blowing up in outrage, they resolutely begin to sift through the debris to see what new things can be made of the broken pieces.

To put it into the idiom of our day—when life hands them a lemon, they make lemonade out of it. The pages of Holy Scripture and of secular history are filled with examples of such positive responses to hardship.

David was a lemonade-maker. He wrote, "I will bless the Lord at all times; His praise shall continually be in my mouth" (Ps. 34:1). David had plenty of reason to complain about life and to become bitter. He faced pressure much greater than most of us will ever see. First, King Saul hunted him week after week. Later David's oldest son, Amnon, committed adultery with his sister. Then David's son Absalom betrayed him and tried to become king. Just before David died, his son Adonijah also tried to grab the throne. Yet David, the man after God's own heart, purposefully chose the pattern and practice of praise in his life rather than the practice of complaining. He said, "Let all those that put their trust in Thee rejoice; let them ever shout for joy, because Thou defendest them; let them also that love

Thy name be joyful in Thee" (Ps. 5:11).

Trials are common to all, but the reactive attitude of praise is not too common. However, it is a choice we can make also.

Jesus was another lemonade-maker. He was no stranger to hardship and disappointment. Again and again what He hoped for and worked to achieve was shattered in failure. Instead of being met with openness and acceptance, He was often met with the kind of hostility and rejection that eventually led to the old rugged cross. If ever a person had a right to complain about injustice and to become cynical toward life, it was Jesus. But He never allowed these experiences to embitter Him or to drive Him to despair. And when He finally died, it was not with a whimper on His lips, but with a victorious shout, "It is finished!"

The Apostle Paul's "prison epistles" are another example of what I am talking about. They comprise not only a sizable portion of the New Testament, but also reveal a creative response to difficult circumstances. No normal or healthy person wants the experience of being put in jail repeatedly, certainly not if you are a religious leader or if you have the kind of aspirations that motivated the Apostle Paul. Therefore, it must have been overwhelmingly frustrating to Paul to be incarcerated again and again in the cities of Asia Minor. How easy it would have been to explode in rage or dissolve in self-pity at such treatment. However, instead of becoming embittered, Paul allowed these circumstances to melt him like flexible wax and shape him in new directions. He found the way not just to endure prison but actually to utilize it in getting on with his objective. Paul did not only make the *best* of a bad situation— he found a way to make the *most* of it.

Never once in any of his writings did he complain about prison life. Never once did he mention the poor food, the deplorable living conditions, or the inhumane treatment of his guards. He rather talked about how God was using his prison experiences to encourage and inspire others to preach more diligently, and how his troubles helped advance the Gospel into new and heretofore unreached areas.

Moreover, Paul chose to use these times of inaction to reflect on the Gospel and correspond with the churches he was birthing and nurturing. Some commentators feel that Paul was such an activist that he would never have taken time to write had it not been for the forced inactivity of imprisonment. Think of what the church throughout ages would have missed if Paul had not set down in writing his understanding of the faith.

Just as a sailor "tacks into the wind" and uses the gusts that are blowing against him to go forward, so Paul used these difficulties of imprisonment to go forward for Christ.

SILENT SUFFERING IN SIBERIA

Georgi Vins is another person who made the best out of life's worst. A pastor of a small Russian Baptist Church, he was exiled to the United States because of his Christian faith. But Georgi Vins had first spent eight years sleeping on a grimy concrete floor next to an open toilet and subsisting on barley extract, tea, and soup in a Russian prison.

While locked deep in the bowels of a Siberian compound, he wrote a diary of his stay, titled *Testament from Prison*. The book contains not one description of prison cruelty, inhumane conditions, or palpable misery that pervades most writings smuggled out of Russian labor camps. Instead, Vins describes the beauty of the Siberian winters, his joy at receiving letters from his wife, his love for Russia, and intimate conversations with God. Except for the title, the book could have been written by a free man living in a penthouse overlooking the Black Sea.

A friend of Vins said, "God knows he deserved to be bitter and full of self-pity, but it is just not there." It is this kind of quiet suffering, Vins believes, that sustains the Christian faith of people in Communist countries. It is most certainly this kind of suffering that marked the early saints.

IN SPITE OF

It is remarkable what people have been able to do while suffering in prison when their responses were right. John Bunyan in Bedford jail wrote *Pilgrim's Progress;* Luther imprisoned in Wartburg Castle translated the entire New Testament into the German language; Dietrich Bonhoeffer wrote *The Cost of Discipleship* while locked in a Nazi prison; the Apostle John, exiled on the Isle of Patmos, wrote the Book of Revelation; and the Apostle Paul, confined in a Roman prison and chained to a guard twenty-four hours a day, still proclaimed the Gospel. Since these men under such mighty handicaps could and did dare to make progress in history, why shouldn't we?

For one's soul there need be no prison walls—no binding chains, no smitten spirit. There are Christians who have learned not to bemoan their troubles or to waste them, but to make slaves of them—people who have learned to use every stumbling stone as material for building a great life. We can do the same thing if we choose to.

THE SECRET

The question could be asked, "How were all of these people able to respond so creatively to hardships and disappointments?" What is the secret of this resilience that enables some people to pick up the pieces and start anew, rather than going to pieces under the impact of tragedy?

The secret lies in how we visualize God's relation to our lives. The problem with Job's wife was that she had a faulty view of God. She had probably been spoiled by the good life and had come to feel that God owed her a trouble-free existence. When this ended, she felt that God was acting unjustly.

God does not promise us such a life nor does He owe us anything. And He is not to blame for every trial that comes to us. Though no event can touch our lives without first passing under the fatherly eye and through the loving hands of God, not everything that happens to us originates solely with God. Some events come straight from God, but others originate from Satan or result from our own wrong decisions and are only permitted by God.

However, the Scriptures teach us that because of God's presence with us—whatever happens to us, either intentionally or permissively, will not be "too much" for us, that is, have the power utterly to destroy us; and some possibility of good will be present in these troubles. God can be counted on for this.

Realizing this can make a tremendous difference in how we cope. If nothing ever occurs without first passing through Him, then we can believe it is not too much, nor is it too late to wrest some good from the wreckage around us.

In the most practical way, this is how we can overcome events rather than being overcome by them. The decision to make lemonade when you find yourself with a lemon on your hands comes from the realization that God is in on your life with you.

Myron Madden was right when he said, "The essence of despair is relegating God solely to the past." We need to believe that God is still at work in the world and in our lives today. His sovereign purpose will ultimately be fulfilled. This hope ought to uplift Christians everywhere. And though pain is not usually a part of His will and does not come directly from His hand, He can use it for our good. Evil is not going to be triumphant forever. Wrong is not always going to win.

As Paul says, every bad thing of life can be transformed by the sovereign power of God if we give that experience to Him (Rom. 8:28). We need to believe this even when we can't see it.

Even when you feel abandoned by God, you need to remember that the feeling and the fact are not the same thing. So if in times of difficulty you feel that your prayers are not getting above the ceiling, don't worry. God can come down below the ceiling. He is not deaf, He is not gone, and He is not limited. He is working silently and redemptively all the while.

Andrew Murray, who lived and died a long time ago, sets out some principles that will help us in facing trials and difficulties in our lives with the right attitude. In times of trouble Andrew Murray suggests that God's trusting child may say:

First: He brought me here;
It is by His will that I am in this strait place; in that will I rest.

Next: He will keep me here in His love, and give me grace in this trial to behave as His child.

Then: He will make the trial a blessing, teaching me the lessons He intends me to learn and working in me the grace He means to bestow.

Last: In His good time He can bring me out again—how and when, He knows.

Say: I am here—
(1) By His appointment.
(2) In His keeping.
(3) Under His training.
(4) For His time.

So, when troubles come, don't give up in despair; don't become angry at God; don't feel sorry for yourself; don't syndicate your sorrows; don't let bitterness consume you. Fight these attitudes and temptations with all of your heart. Above all, don't sin against God with your lips or blame God foolishly.

Actor Walter Hampden, when asked what sentence he considered the most memorable in the English language, quoted from the old Negro spiritual: "Nobody knows the trouble I've seen—glory hallelujah!"

There is splendor in these words. They recognize that human life is full of pain and sorrow and suffering, but they go on to express exultation—the last two words ring with magnificent conviction that the spirit of a Christian enables him to surmount sorrow when he makes the right response to it.

chapter 4
A CASE OF
MISTAKEN IDENTITY

Blaise Pascal once said that it is the fate of God to be everlastingly misunderstood. There is no area of life where this is more common than with the problems of suffering, sorrow, disease, and disaster. When tragedy comes we almost instinctively cry out, "Why has God done this to me?" Or, some well-meaning friend will call what has happened "the will of God." The most horrible of tragedies are labeled "acts of God."

Seriously now, do you believe that the God who created us in His image, who gives us all things richly to enjoy, who identifies Himself as "our Father," and who sent His Son Jesus Christ to die on the cross in our place—do you seriously believe that God is the Author of all the sickness and sorrow of the world?

It is so easy to blame God for all of the world's heartbreak. Could it be that there is a case of mistaken identity? Could it be that He is not the one responsible for the troubles and disasters that creep across our planet? Could it be that we have been blaming the wrong person all along?

The Bible tells us that this is precisely the case. God is not the Author of sorrow and suffering. Calamity is not His deliberate handiwork. Disease is not His making. Don't let anyone confuse you—God is not in the business of trouble-making. If you say that He is, you are blaming sin and evil on God. You are saying He is responsible for the kinds of things that we condemn men for.

Well, if God is not the Author of most of the world's troubles, who is to blame? Read again the classic experience of Job, especially the first two chapters, and you will see. When Job's troubles came, his wife, his friends, and eventually even Job—everybody involved—blamed God. But that was because they did not know any better. They did not have access to all the facts. They could not see behind the scenes.

But we do know better. We have been given the benefit of divine revelation. And one of the lessons of life that we learn from Job is that much of our suffering comes not from God but rather from Satan.

It was not God who troubled Job; it was Satan. It was not God who sent robbers to steal Job's livestock; it was Satan. It was not God who killed Job's servants; it was Satan. It was not God who sent lightning from heaven to burn up Job's sheep; it was Satan. It was not God who sent a violent storm that killed Job's children; it was Satan. It was not God who infected Job's body with sores; it was Satan.

It was God who gave Job all that he had in the first place. It was God who favored him and prospered him. It was God who, when this distressing experience was over, gave Job twice as much as he had before. Why, in heaven's name, would God then have taken it all away from him?

Ultimately, we need to see God not as the cause of our problems, but as the Source of our strength and hope and ability to cope with them. I cannot believe that God reaches down, slightly twists the wheel of a school bus, and watches it crash through a guardrail, killing little children. I cannot believe that God draws a red pencil line through a city and sends a tornado to kill innocent people and leave hundreds homeless. I cannot believe that God jostles the earth, playing with tidal waves, earthquake tremors, and hurricanes, squashing people like ants. I do not believe that God plants cancer in the bone of a little child or a young mother and then stands back with arms folded to watch life slowly waste away.

To believe that God is the Author of all of our troubles is to hold Him responsible for sin and the worst kinds of tragedies. If I believed that about God, then I would want to have nothing to do with Him, nothing whatever. For if this were true He would have less interest in others, less mercy and compassion on them, than I do. No, God is not the one responsible for the troubles of the world. Those who think that He is are suffering from a case of mistaken identity.

JESUS DIDN'T APOLOGIZE

On one occasion Jesus was teaching in the meetinghouse on the Sabbath Day. There was present a woman who had been crippled for eighteen years, and Jesus healed her. He was criticized for healing her on the Sabbath Day. But notice how He defended His action: "Here is a woman, a daughter of Abraham, who has been kept prisoner by Satan for eighteen long years. Was it wrong for her to be freed from her bonds on the Sabbath?" (Luke 13:16, NEB)

Did Jesus apologize to the woman for her illness as though He or God were responsible? Did He blame the physician who had unsuccessfully tried to help her? No. He said that Satan had held her prisoner for eighteen years.

There you have it! There's the guilty party! I think you know by now who it was that first brought trouble to this planet and has been peddling it ever since.

Do you doubt that Satan, not God, is the cause of suffering and sorrow? If so, then study again the story of God's Creation and the Fall in the first three chapters of Genesis. Tragedy, suffering, and death were not a part of God's original plan. These entered the world as a result of sin, and when human nature fell, the physical nature fell also (Gen. 3:17-19). Few of us realize the far-reaching effects of sin on the natural order. When Adam and Eve sinned, all kinds of evil forces were unloosed on the earth. All creation was infected by the sins of people. This accounts for most natural calamities that are labeled "acts of God."

As a result of human rebellion, God's good creation has become a groaning creation (Rom. 8:22). Storms, famine, pestilence, and volcanoes are just the groans and sighs of nature. People's sins put thorns on the roses, fierceness in the beasts, and storms in the wind. But this was not a part of God's original plan.

Do you still have doubts? Look then at the end of time. In heaven there will be no tears, no sorrow, no pain, and no death (Rev. 21:4). This shows that evil and suffering are not a part of God's perfect will for us.

If this is not enough evidence, look at the life and the ministry of Jesus. A great part of Christ's time on earth was spent in healing the sick and diseased. Never once did He turn someone away, saying, "I am sorry, friend. I cannot heal you because God wants you to suffer."

Jesus looked on disease and death as intruders and aliens in God's kingdom. He did not regard God as their Author. Neither should we.

THE GOD OF THIS WORLD

Satan, the author of our troubles, is the god of this world (2 Cor. 4:4). He is presented in Scripture as the opponent of God and the adversary of God's people. It is his purpose to discredit the name of God and to destroy our faith in Him. In the pursuit of this goal he will use anything and anybody he can. He uses bodily pain and afflictions, death and disaster, our children, troubled marriages, and even economic reversals. Whatever irritates and separates, whatever discourages and destroys, Satan will use. His primary purpose is to obstruct and to oppose all that is good and spiritual. He is determined to rob God of His right to rule in the hearts and lives of people and is determined to rob people of the privilege of living in heaven.

Satan has great power and great liberty to do his work, but it is unlimited. He can do nothing without God's permission; yet he has been granted great freedom in doing his work.

He works primarily through deceit and misrepresentation. He is, in fact, the master of deceit, the father of all lies, who masquerades as an angel of light (2 Cor. 11:14). Watch him, as he will come to you under the guise of doing you good when in reality he wants to do you in.

His greatest act of deceit is to convince people that he doesn't even exist. Many people regard Satan as a part of the nursery furniture of history—in the same class as the Easter Bunny, the tooth fairy, and Santa Claus.

Remarkable, isn't it? Second only to the way he deceives us concerning his own existence is the way he uses suffering and sorrow to discredit God. He is so cunning that he causes the sorrow of our world and God gets the blame.

When have you ever heard Satan blamed for tragedy and for disaster? It is always the character of God that is called into question when there is a tragedy or a disaster. Evil and suffering have placed more question marks over the good name of God than anything else in this world. If Satan can cause an accident, give a person cancer, or take the life of a little child in order to discredit God and to destroy our faith, he will gladly do it. And when he does nobody ever cries out, "Why has Satan done this to me?" No one ever labels it as an "act of Satan" and no one ever calls it the "will of the devil." Do you see how cunning, how clever, he is? He causes most of our troubles and God gets the blame.

DON'T BE FOOLED

Though the origin of Satan is shrouded in mystery, his tactics are well known. The Apostle Paul warns us not to be ignorant of his devices (2 Cor. 2:11). We should know not only who he is, and what he is up to, but how he goes about his work. As wise as he is, he has never changed his approaches. Temptation and tribulation are his twin tactics and they are ever the same.

How does Satan work today? For one thing, he creates doubt to lead us to disobedience. Creation had hardly begun when Satan appeared on the scene to raise question marks in the minds of Adam and Eve about the truthfulness of God. By creating doubt he led them into disobedience and punishment.

This disobedience unleashed the forces of evil in the world from which we have not yet recovered. The shock waves are still being felt to the uttermost parts of the earth.

Satan still tries to get us to doubt God's Word so we will sin against Him.

Satan shakes and sifts us to separate us from God. On the night of His betrayal Jesus warned Peter, "Simon, Simon, behold, Satan hath desired to have you, that he may sift you as wheat" (Luke 22:31).

The word *sift* refers to the winnowing process that was used in Jesus' day to separate grain from its husks. Grain was gathered from the field and placed on a stone floor. Then animals were marched around on the grain, and the pressure of their hoofs trampled the kernels from the husks. The farmer, using a wooden shovel, then tossed the grain into the air on a windy day, allowing the wind to blow the lighter husks away and the heavier grain to fall back to the stone floor. By repeating this process again and again, he separated the kernels of grain from their husks.

Jesus warned Peter that that was what Satan wanted to do to him. Satan wanted to shake Peter and his faith in order to separate him from his devotion to the Lord. Satan succeeded temporarily, as he led Peter to deny his Lord that very night.

Years later, out of his own bitter experience Peter writes, "Be sober, be vigilant; because your adversary the devil, as a roaring lion, walketh about seeking whom he may devour" (1 Peter 5:8). Satan was no myth to Peter. And he should not be one to us. The devil, our opponent, is like a ferocious beast prowling around, waiting for an opportunity to destroy us.

Satan also wants to indwell us and make us hypocrites. Barnabas was a generous and a benevolent leader in the New Testament church who sold all of his possessions and gave the entire price of them to the work of God. Others in the church saw his example and were inspired by it. Among them was a couple, Ananias and Sapphira. They too sold their possessions with the intent of giving everything to God and His work. But before they could complete the transaction, Satan entered into their hearts and convinced them that they could just pretend to give everything to the church while keeping a part of it for themselves, and no one would ever know the difference.

The Holy Spirit revealed their deceit to Peter and he confronted them with their sin by asking, "Ananias, why hath Satan filled thine heart to lie to the Holy Ghost . . . ?" (Acts 5:3)

Satan, the great deceiver, wants to lead us into dishonesty, and hypocrisy also, if he can. He will indwell us and make us extensions of his own deceit and evil if we will allow him to do so.

Our own poor judgment, our own deliberate choices—these are the causes of much that distresses us. The Apostle Paul says, "Don't be misled, remember that you can't ignore God and get away with it: a man will always reap just the kind of crop he sows!" (Gal. 6:7, TLB)

You see, if we sow health, we will reap health. If we sow illness, we will reap illness. If we sow trouble, we will reap trouble—every time. We can't sow wild oats all week long and then pray for a crop failure on the weekend.

As a visitor walked through the workshop of a state prison, he passed an inmate who was sewing canvas mailbags for the government. Their eyes met for a brief moment, and the visitor, wishing to be friendly, simply asked, "Sewing?"

"No—reaping," was the sullen reply.

Yes, it works that way—every time. It works with mathematic precision. A person reaps what he sows.

True, Satan is the instigator of evil. But he has not power to force us to do wrong. He can tempt, but he can't make us yield. He can harrass, but he cannot contaminate without our permission. We decide. Lest I be misunderstood let me remind you that though Satan is the ultimate instigator of all evil, he is not the direct cause of *all* our troubles. Some of them we manufacture ourselves. We live in a moral universe where we reap what we have sown.

Other suffering is due to heredity. Some people are born with weaker bodies that are more susceptible to heart attacks, cancer, and other infirmities.

Some sorrow results from the actions of others. We are all free. We can choose our own way in life and those choices often have consequences in the lives of others as well as in our own lives. The good others do splashes on us and so does the evil.

And some suffering is due to the fact that we live in an imperfect world.

But it is all ultimately due to Satan. Though it is true that he is the instigator of evil, he has no power to force us to do wrong. He can tempt but he cannot make us yield. He can harass but he cannot destroy without our permission.

Satan will also hinder us, to prevent us from doing the will of

God. The Apostle Paul wrote to the church at Thessalonica, expressing his desire to visit with them, but he added, "Satan hindered us" (1 Thes. 2:18). The word *hindered* is a technical word which means to throw up a roadblock, to try to stop the progress of an oncoming army. In the days before TNT, tanks, and bazookas, the best ways to retard the progress of an army were to burn the bridges and to create avalanches across its path. In this way an army would be slowed down, hindered in its progress.

The Apostle Paul desired to return to Thessalonica to help those Christians grow to spiritual maturity. But Satan threw up a roadblock that hindered him from doing that. Satan is in the roadblocking business. He will do anything he can to hinder you and me as we try to make progress in Christian service. It is impossible for us to make resolutions about our Christian lives and then to carry out those resolutions without Satan putting obstacles in our way to divert us, to hinder us. If a person resolves to begin a regular devotional life, become an active witness for Christ, and become faithful in church attendance, invariably something will come up. You know what that something is? It's a roadblock placed there by Satan to hinder one from carrying out that resolution, those good intentions.

He is our adversary. Our opponent. And he is going to throw up roadblocks whenever and wherever he can.

And, finally, as in the case of Job, Satan wants to trouble us so we will curse God and reject Him. Satan uses both tribulations and temptations in achieving that purpose.

Remember that Job's suffering did not come from God but from Satan. And it came not because he was bad but because he was good. It was an effort on Satan's part to drive Job to despair. That may well be the reason why trouble has come into your life also.

As Satan brought all kinds of adversity into Job's life, so he will bring adversity into our lives. And if he can get us to blame

God, become bitter against God, and curse God, he has achieved his great purpose.

So the next time sickness, suffering, or tragedy hit you or someone you love, don't be sure that God sent it. Instead of asking, "Why has God done this?" you might ask, "Why did Satan do this?" And if you wonder, "What have I done to deserve this?" the answer might well be, "Nothing. Nothing at all."

Much suffering is the work of Satan, to drive God's people to despair and rejection.

WHY DOESN'T GOD KILL THE DEVIL?

Why, you might wonder, does God allow the devil to continue to do all of these things? If God is stronger than the devil, why doesn't He kill him?

In the story *Robinson Crusoe*, Man Friday asked that very question. Robinson Crusoe answered, "You may as well ask why God doesn't kill you and me when we do wicked things."

The best answer I know to that question is that God has made us like unto Himself, that is, free to make our own choices in life. Choices require options, and options necessitate the existence of the evil one. God does not want us to love Him and serve Him because we have no other choice. He wants us to follow Him because He is our choice.

The only alternative to allowing Satan to exist would be for God to have created us as robots with no choice at all, or as animals with extremely limited choices. But making us in His own image, with the freedom to choose between right and wrong, necessitated Satan's being here.

God will destroy Satan at the end of time—but in the meantime we must contend with him. Until then the Lord will empower us so that neither temptation nor tribulation will overcome us, if we depend on Him.

As Job remained faithful and true to God in the severest times of trial, so we can remain true to God also. We don't have to yield to temptation. We don't have to become bitter, resentful, or angry. We don't have to give in to self-pity. We can have strength immediately and we are assured of victory ultimately.

So the next time trouble comes into your life and you are tempted to say, "Why has God done this to me?" don't! Don't call tragedy the will of God or an act of God when it may not be. Recognize the reality of Satan and give the devil his due.

chapter 5
FINGERTIPS AND POCKET CALCULATORS

Singer Ray Charles was blind by the time he was seven years of age, probably due to glaucoma. He said that when his blindness came he could easily have sunk into apathy and self-pity. What saved him was his mother's courage and intelligence. She simply would not let him do that. She insisted that he become self-sufficient. So she made him scrub the floors, sweep, and even chop wood so that he would not have to depend on other people the rest of his life.

She told him, "You are blind, not stupid. You have lost your eyes, not your mind."

There are many people who when trouble comes focus more on what they've lost than on what they have left. They go through life counting their blessings on their fingertips and their burdens on their pocket calculators. The result is that when real trouble comes, instead of walking through the valley of the shadow of death, they wallow in it. They become victims of despair and they indulge in self-pity.

One of the lessons of life that we learn from Job is that there is a better way to respond to our circumstances. Job teaches us from his rough experiences that God is not some doting grandfather who sits on the edge of heaven, dropping good little gifts out of the sky, saying, "This will make My children happy. This will give them an easy time."

God's goal is not primarily to make us comfortable but to conform us to the image of His Son, Jesus Christ. And in the pursuit of that goal He can and does use all of life's experiences. Even those things that Satan sends to destroy us, God can use to develop us.

This truth confirms what Paul says in Romans 8:28-29: "We know that all things work together for good to them that love God, to them who are the called according to His purpose. For whom He did foreknow, He also did predestinate to be conformed to the image of His Son, that He might be the firstborn among many brethren."

These verses, when rightly understood, are a good foundation for life. They are the basis for hope, confidence, and optimism in Christian living.

But be careful! They do not say that God causes everything; He doesn't. And they do not say that everything that happens is good; it isn't. Nor do they say that everything is going to turn out well for everybody; it won't. And they do not say that everything is working for good as *we* define good; it's not.

The promise is that in spite of suffering and weakness, in spite of persecution and hardships, in spite of anything and everything, God is in control. There is a gracious providence overruling our lives for good. God can turn sickness and misfortune, hardship and persecution, sorrow and death, all of life's experiences, into blessings if we keep on loving Him and want His purpose to be fulfilled in us.

God is at work. And He is never frustrated or defeated, regardless of what may happen in our lives. If we will give Him our lives and all of our experiences, He mixes them together and brings us to the likeness of His dear Son. To do this He uses both what He sends and what He allows. God takes things which Satan intends to use for our destruction and uses them to develop us.

The best illustration of this truth that I know is the baking of a cake. A cake is a combination, a mixture of ingredients. Those ingredients, eaten separately, do not taste very good. In fact, some of them are downright distasteful. But mixed together in the right proportions and under the guidance of a good recipe, something good can come from them. Just so, God can take the distasteful experiences of life and mix them to bring us to a "Masterful" conclusion. If we let Him, He uses what He does not send and He transforms what He does not initiate to make us like Jesus Christ.

With this in mind, the three great truths that Job's experience teaches us about how to live and how to die are: (1) God is more concerned about our character than our comfort. (2) He uses all kinds of experiences to shape us, to mold us, into Christlikeness. (3) Therefore, when life's hardships come to us, instead of sinking into despair and self-pity, we ought to rise to self-improvement; we ought to take a more creative, optimistic, and triumphant view of our difficulties, knowing that God is at work in them.

COMFORT OR CHARACTER?

It is hard for us to understand, and harder still to accept the fact that God is primarily concerned about our character and not our comfort. His goal is not to pamper us physically but to perfect us spiritually.

Charles Colson, ex-hatchet man for President Nixon and founder of Prison Fellowship, has said that he is not proud of the fact that he has been a prisoner. But he agrees with Aleksandr Solzhenitsyn, who after ten years in a Soviet prison, wrote, "Bless you, Prison, bless you for having been my life."

Solzhenitsyn wrote from a prison cell that it was there, lying on rotting prison straw, that for the first time in his life he understood that the purpose of life is not prosperity as we are made to believe, but the maturing of the human soul.

This is true. God is much more concerned with our growth and maturity than He is with our happiness.

We are the opposite. Our primary concern is our comfort and ease. But God knows that comfort is temporary whereas character is permanent. We may be comfortable today and in total misery tomorrow. Material and physical things can be gone in an instant. In fact, last week the home of the mother of one of my friends was completely destroyed when a spark ignited a gas leak in her house, and her life was almost lost. My friend told me, "In just three seconds she lost what it took her fifty years to accumulate."

In an instant our whole lives can be changed. But character is abiding. It can't be destroyed that easily. Knowing that, God majors on character and not on comfort.

God is not simply interested in saving our souls; He wants to develop a Christlike character in us. Christian character is not something we inherit or something that is given to us. It is something that we develop. And it does not come cheaply. Developing Christian character almost always involves suffering. Through life's experiences and our response to them, character is built. Troubles and hardships mixed with faith make us into the kind of people we ought to be.

The measuring rod of Christian maturity is Jesus Christ Himself. One of the greatest American sculptors was Gutzon Borglum, who died in 1941. He made the great carving of the heads of Washington, Jefferson, Lincoln, and Theodore Roosevelt on Mt. Rushmore in South Dakota. At one time he worked for many months on a six-ton block of marble. A woman who cleaned his studio every day wondered what the great block was for. Finally after much toil features began to emerge from the marble. When the cleaning woman saw them, she exclaimed, "How did Mr. Borglum know that Abraham Lincoln was in that stone?"

How did the Lord know that Jesus Christ could be seen in you and me, rough blocks that we are? He knew because He planted His likeness in us when He saved us. And now He keeps chiseling on us until someone recognizes that Christ lives in us.

Have you learned that in the victories of life we should celebrate and in the defeats of life we should evaluate? When we are victorious we want to have a party and enjoy ourselves. But when we are defeated we back off and examine ourselves. We try to determine what went wrong and what we can do to change the situation next time. This is as true spiritually as it is athletically.

HOT-WATER CHRISTIANS

The second thing I want you to see is that adversity is one of the tools that God uses to shape us. Difficulties are often God's way to victory. Character is seldom developed in places of comfort and ease.

If by an act of grace God directs your life in easy and pleasant paths, then thank Him for that and use those advantages for His glory. But few of us will find life that way.

Christians should be like photographs of Christ, and the finest likenesses of Him are developed in the darkroom of sorrow and affliction. The Christian life is not all gravy, joy, and light. There are those who call themselves Christians that promise us health and wealth if we will just become their kind of Christians—and send in our offerings. Their motto is: "Name it and claim it." Ask for it and it's yours.

That kind of faith will not stand either the test of time or the test of adversity. The Christian life is not all health and wealth.

It is not all name it and claim it. God knows that we must be chiseled by hardships and adversities if the image of Jesus Christ is to emerge in us.

James wrote about this perfecting process: "My brethren, count it all joy when you fall into various trials, knowing that the testing of your faith produces patience. But let patience have its perfect work, that you may be perfect and complete, lacking nothing" (James 1:2-4, NKJV).

James prescribed an uncommon way of looking at and responding to the common problems of life because he saw that God has a definite purpose in all that He allows to come into our lives.

Trials, according to James, develop patience in us. Patience is strength of character. It is the ability to stand up to life without going to pieces or going to a liquor bottle. God uses hardships to make us tough. And this moral and spiritual toughness is an essential part of Christian maturity. So God's perfecting process is this: pressures produce patience and patience leads to perfection. It is only as we suffer that we become strong. And it is only as we are strong that we become mature. So our trials are not to punish us but to perfect us. They are not to make us miserable but to make us mature.

Years ago, after a blacksmith had given his heart to God, he was approached by an intellectual unbeliever with this question: "Why is it that you have so much trouble? I've been watching you. Since you joined the church and began to walk square and seem to love everybody, you have twice as many trials and accidents as you had before. I thought that when a man gave himself to God, his troubles were over."

With a thoughtful but glowing faith, the blacksmith replied, "Do you see that piece of steel? It is for the springs of a wagon, but it needs to be tempered. In order to do this, I heat it red-hot, and then cool it with water. If I find that it will take a temper, I heat it again; then hammer it and bend it and shape it so that it will be suitable for the wagon. Often I find the steel too brittle, and it cannot be used. If this is so, I throw it on the scrap heap. Those scraps are worth less than one cent a pound; but this wagon spring is valuable.

He paused a moment and his listener nodded. Then the blacksmith continued: "God saves us for something more than to have a good time. At least, that is the way I see it. We have a good time, all right, for the smile of God means heaven. But He wants us for service, just as I want this piece of steel. And He puts the 'temper' of Christ in us by the testings and trials which come our way. He also supplies the strength to meet these testings.

"Since I have learned this, I have been saying to Him: 'Test me in any way You choose, Lord—only don't throw me on the scrap heap.' "

Much as carbon, under the tremendous pressure of tons of earth, in time produces a beautiful diamond, and as iron under the tremendous heat and pressure of the furnace produces steel, so God allows our character to be formed under the pressure and heat of circumstances. It is only as we suffer that we grow into the beauty and the strength of Christ.

When a football coach wants to build a good team, he does not send his players out on the field to play with soft pillows. He puts them to work against rough opponents, a bucking frame, and a tackling dummy, and he puts them through exercises that are strenuous. God does the same thing with us. To give us the strength of steadfastness and patience in our character, He pits us at times against tough opponents, against temptations, against public opinion, against discouragements, and against trials.

The Lord often allows us to go through painful experiences and endure hardships because these are the things that develop us into the kind of people we need to be. God allows some suffering and some difficulties because there are some things to be accomplished in our character that can be brought about only by this means (1 Peter 1:7).

Great civilizations and great people are not made that way by soft living but by challenges and their responses to those challenges. Great Christians are made in the same way.

Someone has said, "A Christian is like a tea bag—not worth very much until he gets into some hot water." The hot water experiences of life do have a way of bringing out the best that is within us.

Remember that a pearl begins as a pain in the stomach of an oyster. A grain of sand or some sharp cutting substance becomes lodged in the body of the oyster, perhaps between the soft tissue and the shell. It is not only irritating, but painful. Since it cannot be expelled, the most precious substance that the oyster produces is deposited around the irritating, foreign body. This process continues until the source of the irritation becomes a beautiful pearl. Without the pain and suffering, there would be no pearl. With little irritation, there would be only a tiny one, but with much suffering, there is a large, luminous one.

If our lives flowed along smoothly and easily, we might be sweet and gentle creatures, but without much strength of character and with no pearls. Overcoming hardships, withstanding temptation, and neutralizing irritations and suffering with pearl-stuff are what makes lives strong and beautiful.

Why does God permit suffering in the world? Perhaps it is the only way to develop strength and to make pearls.

An unknown poet has put it this way:

> *When God wants to drill a man,*
> *And thrill a man,*
> *And skill a man,*
> *When God wants to mold a man*
> *To play the noblest part;*

When He yearns with all His heart
To create so great and bold a man
That all the world shall be amazed,
Watch His methods, watch His ways!
How He ruthlessly perfects
Whom He royally elects!
How He hammers him and hurts him
And with mighty blows converts him
Into trial shapes of clay which
Only God understands;
While his tortured heart is crying
And he lifts beseeching hands!
How he bends but never breaks
When his good He undertakes;
How He uses whom He chooses,
And with every purpose fuses him;
By every act induces him
To try his splendor out—
God knows what He's about!

God knows that in you there is the potential to be like Christ. And if pressure or irritation, or if hot water or chiseling, can bring it out, then He will use them to accomplish His purpose.

Are you then ready to accept adversity as well as blessings? Can you take hardships and difficulties without indulging in self-pity or complaining against God? Do you recognize that God has a right to bring the unpleasant as well as the pleasant into your life? Without this concept, you will never be able to persevere through pressure. It will blow you away!

IT'S FUN TO FEEL SORRY FOR YOURSELF

Since it is true that God is more concerned about our character than our comfort, and since God can and does use all of life's experiences, those He sends as well as those He allows, to develop that character, then we ought not to give in to self-pity when trouble comes. We ought to stand up to life victoriously and hopefully, with confidence and assurance, refusing to allow circumstances to beat us down and defeat us.

Last night my wife asked, "What are you preaching about tomorrow?"

I said, "I am going to preach on Job again."

"What are you going to say about him this time?" she asked.

I replied, "I am going to say that Job teaches us not to feel sorry for ourselves."

And she said, "I don't want to go! I want to feel sorry for myself."

It feels good to feel sorry for yourself once in a while. And a little of that is OK. Just don't take it too far. Don't wallow in the valley of self-pity. Walk through it. And walk through it with confidence and courage because the Lord said that He would be by your side all the while.

Do you really believe Romans 8:28 and James 1:2-4? Do you believe that God is at work in all the circumstances of your life, to make you more Christlike? Sometimes it is not easy to accept that. Paul did *not* say, "We *understand* that all things work together for good." And he did not say, "We *see* how all things work together for good." To the believer he said, "We *know* that they do." We know of many things that we do not understand and we cannot see at the moment. We know by faith that they are true. We consciously believe this even when we cannot see it or prove it or understand it. God is intermingling all things for our good. Nothing will save us from self-pity like believing this.

You can believe this because God said it. And when life seems to be tumbling in around you, you can be sure that God is there—chiseling, hammering, heating the water, and pressuring you to make you more perfect.

Listen, I have lived long enough to thank God for my trials

and my troubles. What I thought at one time was the benediction of my ministry turned out to be the invocation. What seemed to be the worst thing that could happen to me has turned out to be the best thing.

That's why I refuse to feel sorry for myself. That's why I keep looking beyond the moment to see God at work. As a kite rises highest against the wind, so I want to let the troubles of my life carry me to new heights with God.

Since this is true, don't spend your life counting your blessings on your fingertips and your burdens on your pocket calculator. Don't wallow in self-pity. The posture of a Christian in today's world ought to be "knees down and chin up." The wonderful promises of God ought to make us beautiful and not bitter—gracious and not grumpy—cheerful and not complaining. That's the way to live—and to die.

chapter 6
LIFE IN A NUTSHELL

Philosopher Sidney J. Hook once said, "Any philosophy that can be put in a nutshell should be." His words are a warning to those who try to give neat, simple answers to life's complex problems. This word of caution is especially needed when we try to explain evil and suffering—why the worst of things often happen to the best of people.

Of course we want to know why. God gave us an inquiring mind and it is natural for us to ask questions. But one of the lessons of life we learn from Job is that we must learn to live without answers.

When Job's troubles came to him and he cried out for an answer, his friends came up with a few answers. But their answers did not satisfy Job.

The approach that God took with Job was the direct opposite of what these friends had tried. God made no attempt to "explain" the process of tragedy to Job, and this for two very obvious reasons. First, Job was in no position to understand ultimate answers, even if they had been given him, for they belong to the realm of the infinite, and he was just a finite creature. Frederick Buechner says explaining everything to Job would be like trying to explain Newtonian physics to a small-necked crab. The capacity of the one is simply not equal to the immensity of the other.

The fact is that as human beings "we know in part" and "we see through a glass darkly" (1 Cor. 13:12). To ask to understand the "whys" of life is to ask more than is possible for us to understand.

Augustine of Hippo once said, "The Almighty does nothing without reason, but the frail mind of man cannot always explain the reason." We therefore should not expect total understanding of life and its experiences and God is under no obligation to let us in on His plans.

There is another reason why God did not attempt to clarify Job's situation with lots of answers. It is because explanations were really not what Job needed most at that moment. What if he had been given all the facts? What if God had explained to Job down to the last detail why those economic reversals had taken place, and why that tornado had swept away his whole family, and why his body was now covered with boils? A total array of such facts would not have resolved anything, for even if Job had possessed all of this knowledge, the task of accepting these facts and learning to live in the light of them would still have been before him. The pain would still be there to be borne hour after hour, the empty chairs around the breakfast table would still have to be faced every morning, and the problem of having no money would still have to be contended with. What Job needed was not abstract explanations of his plight. He needed to know how to cope with his circumstances, how to go on living with what had happened.

George Buttrick was right in saying that life is essentially a series of events to be borne and lived through rather than intellectual riddles to be played with and solved. Life is not to be explained; it is to be lived. The Lord knows that, which probably is why He never bothered to give Job answers to his struggles.

What Job needed was someone to share with, to assure him that he had not been forgotten or abandoned, that there was still a future, no matter how mangled the past and the present had become. What he needed was "grace sufficient," not "to know it all" but to "bear it all." And that is what God gave him.

Therefore, nowhere in the Book of Job is there an attempt by God to explain things fully to this suffering man, or to any of us. But God did assure him that he was not alone or abandoned or forsaken, but that He was by Job's side. God did not give him an answer; that would not be enough. Instead He gave Himself as the answer—His companionship, His courage, His hope. And that, my friend, is worth more than a thousand answers and ten thousand reasons.

What Job needed was strength. So God became His Strength. What Job needed was redemption. So God became His Redeemer. What Job needed was hope. So God became his Hope. The only answer God gave Job in his trials was Himself. He said, "Job, I am with you and I am all you need."

In his trials Job gained a new understanding of God and he discovered as we need to discover that our ultimate need is not explanations as to why things happen, but the ability to cope with them.

STABILIZER OR TRANQUILIZER

What we need most in the hour of trouble is not a tranquilizer but a stabilizer, not something to calm us down but someone to shore us up; not a way of escape but the ability to cope; not something to steady our nerves but someone to strengthen our feet. The Lord does that for us. Jude describes God as the One who "is able to keep you from falling" (Jude 24).

In times of trial God becomes our Strength and keeps us on

our feet. In fact, three times in Scripture God promises to make
our feet like hinds' feet (2 Sam. 22:34; Ps. 18:33; Hab. 3:19).
A hind is a mountain-climbing deer known for its surefooted-
ness. As it climbs the treacherous mountain paths, its strong
and steady feet keep it from falling. Just so, God makes our feet
steady and strong as we travel through life.

God does not promise to keep us from the slippery slopes or
from dangerous pathways in life. What He promises is to be
with us and give us sure feet so that we do not stumble and fall
to destruction. He promises, "I will be with you and I will be
your Strength."

Whenever God says a thing once we need to pay attention to
it. But when He takes time to say it three times, then we really
need to take heed to it. The truth is that God strengthens us and
sustains us by His grace in the difficult experiences of life so
that they do not defeat us.

Isaiah spoke of the Lord's being our Strength when he wrote,
"Hast thou not known? Hast thou not heard, that the everlasting
God, the Lord, the Creator of the ends of the earth, fainteth not,
neither is weary? There is no searching of His understanding.
He giveth power to the faint; and to them that have no might He
increaseth strength. Even the youths shall faint and be weary,
and the young men shall utterly fall; but they that wait upon the
Lord shall renew their strength; they shall mount up with wings
as eagles, they shall run, and not be weary; and they shall
walk, and not faint" (Isa. 40:28-31).

This is a definite promise of divine strength that comes to us
in three different forms. It comes to us in the form of ecstasy, in
the form of inspiration, and in the form of endurance. Sometimes God's strength comes to us in such a way that we mount
up on wings of eagles, and we soar above the problems and the
difficulties of life. There are times when God gives us such joy
and happiness that it is comparable only to the soaring of an
eagle. This is a real hope, a real promise, a gift from God. But

we must be careful lest we think that committing our lives to Christ will solve all of our problems and make us soar all the time. That simply is not true.

Sometimes God's strength comes to us in the form of inspiration. We will run and not become weary. This is another kind of help that God often gives to us. He motivates us, inspires us, and empowers us to get through our troubles and trials. The job is done with speed and with strength.

But many times the strength of God comes to us in the form of endurance. Oftentimes in life we are slowed down to a walk. All we can do is just trudge along. We are not soaring as eagles and we are not running as racers; we are just shuffling along. But to walk without fainting is good news. Just to hang in there, to endure, to be patient is also a gift of God's grace.

Some people think that Isaiah's order is all turned around in these verses. They say that soaring should be last. Not so! God knew what He was talking about when He led Isaiah to set things in this order. The most difficult discipline is not to soar like an eagle or to run like a racer, but to keep on keeping on.

This passage is a promise of grace for all the gears of life— the high gear of flying, the middle gear of running, and the low gear of walking.

LIVING WITHOUT ANSWERS

God is not only our Strength; He is also our Redeemer. As we go through troubles He undergoes them with us and works in us to redeem both them and us for His glory.

Joseph's life is a case in point. Joseph was one of the good and godly men of the Old Testament. Yet he suffered all kinds of trials and injustices. Being good did not exempt him from trouble; instead, it caused much of his trouble.

When Joseph was still a teenager his brothers took him by force and sold him as a slave to a traveling caravan. Joseph's father had always showed favoritism toward him because he was Rachel's firstborn son. He gave Joseph the easy jobs to do around the house and when there were new clothes to be bought Joseph got them and his brothers got the hand-me-downs. The jealousy of his brothers grew to resentment and finally to such intense hatred that they sold Joseph into slavery and then lied to their father, saying that Joseph had been killed by wild beasts.

As Joseph was being transported down to Egypt as a slave he must have wondered, "Where is God? Why has He allowed this to happen to me? How is all of this fitting into His plan for my life?" It would have been easy for Joseph to have become angry toward both God and his brothers for what was happening to him. But Joseph refused to allow bitterness and self-pity to consume him. There is no evidence that he harbored any of these feelings.

Once he was in Egypt, he was sold to Potiphar, captain of the Pharaoh's guard. Joseph worked hard, and kept a good attitude, and the Lord prospered him. In time Potiphar made Joseph the overseer of his large household. Joseph was now the top man in the household of one of the top government officials of Egypt.

Joseph had a lot of things going for him. He was young, handsome, intelligent, and he was always around. This was not true of Potiphar. He was usually gone on government business. Mrs. Potiphar was lonely and she was soon attracted to Joseph. One day she made a sexual advance toward him. But Joseph had such a high regard for his master and such deep devotion to God that he rejected her. Angered and hurt at Joseph's rejection, she falsely accused him of the very thing he had refused to do. Potiphar believed his wife and, acting on circumstantial evidence, had Joseph thrown in prison.

How much should one man have to take? First, despised by his brothers through no fault of his own, and now thrown into prison on trumped-up charges. It just wasn't fair! Where was

God in all of this? Surely Joseph had a right to complain and to feel sorry for himself. God, from all appearances, was not treating him right. But there is no evidence that Joseph held any of these destructive feelings.

In prison he was a model prisoner and soon became a trusty. He was constantly befriending and helping other prisoners in every way possible. He was even instrumental in helping at least one of them gain his freedom. Joseph helped the butler of the king in this way. The butler promised that as soon as he was free he would do whatever he could to help Joseph in return. But once released he promptly forgot his promise and Joseph was left to languish in jail.

That would have been enough to break anyone. Here was Joseph, a man wanting to serve God, trying to do right, but everything weny wrong. He was mistreated by his own brothers, falsely accused by his boss's wife, and now forgotten by a man he had befriended. Nobody would have blamed Joseph if he had become bitter and resentful at all of that. That would be enough to cause anyone to feel sorry for himself. But once again there is no hint of any of these feelings in Joseph. None at all.

Finally, Joseph was released from prison. Partly because of his positive attitude and optimistic spirit he once again earned the favor of his superiors. He was eventually made the Secretary of Agriculture for all of Egypt and in that position he was able to lead the nation in a program of food production and conservation that would carry them through seven years of the severest famine that they had ever experienced.

Later Joseph was reunited with his brothers who had sold him into slavery years before. They expected, as we would expect, that Joseph would be bitter and vengeful toward them. They assumed that anger had been festering in him throughout all of these years and he would be just waiting for a chance to get even. So it was with fear and trembling that Joseph's brothers met with him.

But Joseph surprised everyone with his response. Instead of being angry at them, he told them not to be grieved or angry with themselves for, he said, "God sent me before you to preserve you a posterity in the earth, and to save your lives by a great deliverance. So now it was not you that sent me hither, but God; and He made me a father to Pharaoh, and lord of all his house, and a ruler throughout all the land of Egypt" (Gen. 45:7-8).

Joseph's brothers could not believe that he had come through all of his misfortune with such a gracious and loving spirit. They still feared that he would seek revenge for the obvious injustices he had suffered. So Joseph reassured them by saying, "Fear not, for am I in the place of God? But as for you, ye thought evil against me, but God meant it unto good, to bring to pass, as it is this day, to save much people alive" (Gen. 50:19-20).

As Joseph looked back on his life he saw the hand of God working in both the good and the bad things that he had experienced. God had used all that had happened to him, the evil as well as the good, for a redemptive purpose. What his brothers had intended as harm, God had turned into help for thousands.

No one would disagree that if ever a person had a right to complain, be bitter, or be filled with self-pity, it was Joseph. But he refused to allow these feelings to destroy him. Joseph took a wrong done to him by his brothers and turned it into feeding starving Egypt and the very brothers who had sold him into slavery. Joseph might have eaten his heart out, chewing on his resentments. But instead he turned a wrong into a glorious right. It was because he saw God as his Redeemer in and through all of this that he could keep such a positive spirit.

As God was Joseph's Redeemer, so He is our Redeemer also, if we trust Him. Usually it is only as we look back, that we see this and the meaning of many things that baffle us in the present. We do not know how to read the true meaning of what is happening now. That is why we must learn to take our burdens to the Lord and leave them there and not become bitter when the storms of life come.

A LOT TO GIVE ACCOUNT FOR

One thing more: God promises to be our Hope also. There are really two faulty positions we can take in the face of the mystery of evil and suffering. First, we can demand "total intellectual understanding." I have already pointed out that this is presumptuous and asking for more than anyone can know.

The second position is just as unacceptable. It is to "accept life with unquestioning resignation."

If I have been told once, I have been told a hundred times: "We must not question God. We must not try to understand. We have no right to ask or to inquire into the ways of God with men. The way out is to submit. We must silently and totally surrender. We must accept what God does without a word of murmur."

As a leaf submits to the wind without a word, and as a rock allows the floodwater to do whatever it pleases without murmur, some people say we should yield unquestioningly to God. But I cannot accept this for it reduces all of life to a mechanical power transaction.

Where did some Christians get the notion that we must not question God or have any right to pour out our souls to Him and ask "Why?" It certainly does not come from the Scriptures. The approach of unquestioning resignation comes closer to pagan stoicism that to Christian humility.

In a time of national distress Gideon cried out, "If the Lord be with us, why then is all this befallen us?" (Jud. 6:13) Habakkuk the prophet saw evil triumphing and righteousness oppressed and cried out to God, "Why?" (Hab. 1:3) Even Jesus on the cross cried, "My God, My God, why . . . ?" (Mark 15:34) And Job, in the midst of his agony, attempted to interrogate the Almighty as to why he was going through all of his trials.

John Claypool, a fellow pastor, says that shortly before his eleven-year-old daughter died with leukemia he received a letter from his friend Carlyle Marney. Dr. Marney admitted that he had no word for the suffering of the innocent, and never had. But he wrote, "I fall back on the idea that God has a lot to give an account for."

That may sound shocking to you at first, but the more you reflect on it the more I think you will agree that he is right. God holds us responsible for our actions and I believe He expects us to hold Him responsible for His. And when all the facts are in, when the last ripple of our lives reaches the farthest shore of eternity, God will give us such an accounting. Until then, it is valid to ask.

But God can be trusted. He knows that we need answers and he promises that one day He will give them to us. The Apostle Paul wrote, "For now we see through a glass darkly, but then face to face. Now I know in part, but then shall I know even as also I am known" (1 Cor. 13:12).

This verse is a teaching in contrast. Note the words *now* and *then* are each used twice. The word *now* refers to the present time. The word *then* refers to heaven. In the present our knowledge is partial and incomplete, but in heaven it will be direct and comprehensive.

The word *glass* refers to a mirror. In New Testament days mirrors were not made of glass with quicksilver on the back as they are today. They were made of polished metal. Instead of giving a clear reflection, they gave one that was distorted at best. Paul used the illustration of a mirror to show the limited, distorted understanding that people have of things in this life. But he promised us that if we keep on believing in God and keep on trusting Him, one of these days He will explain all things to us.

In heaven there will be question-and-answer times and everyone will leave satisfied. One day God will explain all the mysteries of life to us. In the meantime we must trust Him.

Regardless of what your question may be, answer-time is coming after we get to heaven. That's a promise from Him and you can bank on it. But until then we must trust Him.

As it was with Job, so it is with us. God does not give us answers. He gives us Himself as the answer and that is enough. Helen Bagby Harrison, in a biographical account of her parents who were pioneer missionaries to Brazil, writes of the death of her mother. As Helen and her mother boarded a plane on their way to a family reunion they found that the pilot was an old friend. As they settled back in their seats, Mrs. Bagby remarked, "My, but it's good to know the pilot."

Shortly after being airborne Mrs. Bagby leaned back in her seat and died. It is the same with us. If we know the Pilot, it is enough. Knowing the Pilot does not keep us out of the turbulence of life. But it does keep the turbulence out of us.

To know the Pilot is enough. God is the Answer. He is our Strength; He is our Redeemer; He is our Hope; He is enough.

chapter 7
THE ELOQUENCE OF SILENCE

God's dealings with Job teach us that life is not to be explained; it is to be lived. That's why Job was left to struggle with his suffering and sorrow with no answers from God.

If God did not explain to Job why he was suffering, don't you think it is rather presumptuous for us to try to explain to our friends why they are suffering? If God gave no answer to Job for the seeming injustices of life, but rather gave Himself as the answer, doesn't this suggest that the best thing we can give our friends in their sorrow and suffering is not an explanation but ourselves?

It has been my experience that neither learned nor lengthy answers help much in times of trouble. The question, "Why is God doing this to me?" is not really a theological question; it is a cry of pain. It is not usually a request for information but rather an invitation for God to do something to make the victim of injustice or misfortune feel better.

Times of crises, suffering, and grief are golden opportunities to reach out and help people if we know what to do and how to do it. One lesson of life we learn from Job, by example and by contrast, is how to minister to grieving and troubled friends.

When Job's friends learned about his misfortunes they immediately went to be with him and to comfort him in his distress. When they saw his countenance disfigured almost beyond recognition by the painful boils, they lifted up their voices and wept for him. Then for seven days and seven nights they sat on the ground with him and did not say one word. Job's grief was so great that they simply sat with him in silent suffering.

In this experience we have an example of how to minister to our grieving friends. Job's friends did three things to help him in his sorrow:

1. They went to him.
2. They wept for him.
3. They waited with him.

This initial ministry of Job's three friends shows us how we may help our grieving friends.

MAKE YOURSELF AVAILABLE

The first thing Job's friends did on hearing of his trouble was to go and be with him. That's the first thing we ought to do also.

"But," you tell me, "I feel so inadequate. I don't know what to say." Don't let that stop you. We all feel helpless at a time like that. I have been trying to minister to people in trouble and in grief for almost thirty years and I still feel inadequate.

It helped me when I finally realized that I do not need to say anything at all. Why do we feel we must say something to give immediate relief to those under stress? What our grieving friends do not need is an instant sermon or a simple answer or a long Scripture quotation. What they need is us—our concern, our presence, and our love. This means more than any words we might say. Answers do not heal broken hearts. Explanations do not soothe troubled spirits. Only God, friends, and time can do that.

I know of a woman who lost her husband in an automobile accident. When her pastor heard of the tragedy he immediately went to be with her. When word of the death came to her Sunday School teacher, she went to be with the lady also. And as the church received news of the death, several members went one by one to take food and to sit with her.

By God's grace and through their ministry in time her broken heart healed and the Lord gave her another husband. But as happens sometimes, this marriage did not work out and her second husband left her. This time no one came to minister to her—not the pastor, not the Sunday School teacher, not any church members—no one.

As she shared her hurt with her Sunday School teacher some months later she said, "When my first husband died the pastor came, you came, and many from the church came. But when I lost my second husband no one came—and he was just as gone, and I was just as lonely."

Her teacher replied, "But we didn't know what to say." The lady replied, "That's strange; you didn't know what to say when I lost my first husband either, but you came anyhow and that's what counted."

People need people. And in the hour of need, whether it's due to a death or a divorce or the diagnosis of a dreaded disease, we can give our friends no greater gift than the gift of ourselves.

HELP YOUR FRIENDS EXPRESS THEIR GRIEF

A second thing Job's friends did in ministering to him was to weep with him. The fact that they lifted up their voices and wept suggests that they actually entered into Job's experience of grief with him. They felt what he felt. They shared his deep sorrow. They wept and allowed him to weep also.

To help a friend in grief, you need to be the kind of person with whom the griever can weep unashamedly, knowing that you are suffering with him. The emotion of grief may be expressed or repressed. If we are wise, we will express grief. One of the best ways to do this is through tears. In contemporary society there is considerable pressure to suppress grief. Have you felt or do you feel that pressure?

For example, it may be considered all right to be happy, even to laugh—if not too loud. But many think that it is not all right to weep. Our society puts a premium on stoic concealment of emotions, particularly those caused by or related to death.

The pressure to suppress emotions begins for many in the early years. This is particularly true for boys. How frequently have you heard someone say, "Big boys don't cry"? What a terrible injustice we do to boys when we teach them not to cry. Some of those boys grow up to be big men who cannot cry when they need to do so.

Contrary to what many people seem to believe, the expression of grief is a normal and a healthy experience. It has even been suggested that giving expression to grief, through tears or otherwise, is the "best available mental health insurance." More and more the medical profession is coming to believe that one of the reasons there are more old ladies around than there are old men is that women learn early in life that it is OK to weep.

The Jews have a proverb that says, "Tears are to the soul what soap is to the body." Tears have a cleansing and a healing effect. In fact one of God's greatest gifts for our health and our healing is the ability to cry.

Unfortunately, tears are sometimes equated with weakness. They are not a sign of weakness, however; nor are they an evidence of a lack of faith. King David was not a weakling. He was a "man after [God's] own heart" (Acts 13:22). And yet, when word came to David that Absalom, his rebel son, had been killed, he "went up to the chamber over the gate and wept" (2 Sam. 18:33). In one of the most memorable laments known to man David cried, "O, my son Absalom, my son, my son Absalom! Would God I had died for thee, O Absalom my son, my son!" (18:33)

Jesus was certainly no weakling and was not lacking in faith, and yet He wept over Jerusalem (Luke 19:41). He also wept with Mary at the grave of His friend Lazarus (John 11:35).

Benjamin Disraeli once said, "Never apologize for showing feelings. Remember that, when you do, you apologize for the truth." We are emotional, feeling beings and it is not wrong to express those emotions, even with tears. It is in fact good when we do.

We can do nothing finer for friends than to weep with them and allow them to weep also.

THE ELOQUENCE OF SILENCE

The third thing Job's friends did to minister to him was to wait with him. They sat on the ground with him for seven days and nights, and during this time they did not say a word, because they saw how utterly grief-stricken he was.

It would have been best (so far as the comforting process was concerned) if the story had ended there. But unfortunately it did not. After Job began to complain about his situation, his friends spoiled it all by trying to give him intellectual answers to life. They missed the opportunity to go down in history as uniquely sensitive and understanding men because they wouldn't keep quiet.

It is the unanimous testimony of sufferers the world over that words do not help much in a time of grief. On the contrary they often hurt. One of the most important lessons for us to learn about how to help others in the grieving process is to learn that it is usually futile and unproductive to try to explain their tragedy in some comprehensive way. We are most likely to be helpful with an economy of words. It is awfully easy to say too much, to talk when we ought to listen.

In ministering to grieving friends there is nothing quite as eloquent as silence. To be with them, to weep for them, to wait on them, is enough.

WHAT NOT TO SAY

A recent "Dear Abby" letter tells us what not to say. A lady wrote to Abby that her fourteen-year-old son had been killed in a tragic accident several months earlier and that she was just beginning to come out of the numbness and the shock. Throughout the ordeal, friends, family, and acquaintances had tried to comfort her. Some succeeded while others failed miserably.

In her letter she said, "The following comments are words that did not help at all. I realize that everyone was trying to be kind, but there are certain words bereaved parents do not want to hear:

"1. *I know just how you feel. I lost my mother, father, husband, brother, sister, etc.* These words are so shallow to a parent who has lost a child. Unless they have suffered the loss of a child, there is no way on earth they can know how you feel.

"2. *It was God's will.* I am no more (or less) religious than the average person, but if it was God's will to take my son at fourteen and end his young life, then I want no part of a God who could be so cruel.

"3. *God needed him more than you did.* How inadequate that made me feel, as though something was lacking within myself. If I had needed him more, would he still be alive?

"4. *These things happen for a reason.* What reason? There is no reason good enough to explain why I have to suffer the loss of my child.

"*You can have another child, or at least you have your other children*. That is really cold and cruel. Children are individuals and no child can replace the child who has died.

"Now for some words that comforted me: a simple and heartfelt, *I'm so sorry*. Many people hugged me, held my hand, or cried with me. No words were spoken, but they were there for me when I needed them.

Linda in Lancaster"

Friends, take note! When ministering to a grieving friend we should avoid the temptation to give simple, trite, and easy answers to the complex questions of life. The ministry of silence is usually of much greater value than the ministry of words to the brokenhearted.

So to best help your grieving friend, just be a friend. And if anyone must talk, let it be the friend. You listen. Listen without offering explanations and without passing judgment. Many problems can be solved by letting your friend talk. One reason why sharing verbally so frequently helps is that it enables him to filter through his own thinking and see things more clearly. Telling frequently relieves tensions. Fears and anxieties lessen and sometimes disappear entirely as they are told to a sympathetic listener.

We need to minister to one another, and one of the best ways is by being the kind of friend who listens. We, the church, are the body of Christ on earth today. As Jesus ministered to people in grief, so we should minister to them. His experience in ministering to Mary and Martha at the death of Lazarus stands as an example to us. What did Jesus do at that time? First He went, He wept, and He waited. We can do the same thing for our friends—a touch, a hug, a sympathetic smile is enough. Our presence says volumes about how much we care.

There is simply no substitute for good friends. Our conversations with people can be divided into three categories: facts, opinions, and emotions. Of course, all talk contains a certain amount of all three, but in a true friendship our talk moves from facts to opinions to emotions. New acquaintances usually restrict their conversation to facts. Then they begin to trust each other with their opinions. And finally, after they have become genuine friends, emotions begin to emerge. That's what we need to share—our emotions—which include those deep feelings of life that can destroy us if we do not get rid of them.

FIVE DEADLY EMOTIONS

There are at least five emotions which comprise the grief that we need to share with others, or we need to bear with others in order for healing to come:

1. The first is shock and surprise. When death comes suddenly, it can be like a hammer blow. But even if a death has been expected, when it finally happens the bereaved can almost feel it physically when informed of the news. Instinctively, he may deny it. "Oh, no" he may say, because he cannot take it in. At that point, numbness takes place almost as though an anesthetic has been administered. Usually there is also an emotional release, and the bereaved breaks down and weeps. In grief, the shock and numbness may be so serious that he is unaware of what is going on around him.

2. As the numbness begins to wear off, life may become terrifying. C.S. Lewis said upon experiencing the death of his wife, "No one ever told me that grief felt so like fear."

Yesterday a lady who regularly views our television ministry called me long distance to tell me how these messages from Job had helped her. A year ago her husband died of a brain tumor. Since that time she has been so anxious, so nervous, so tense that she has not been able to do many of the ordinary things that she could do before, such as drive an automobile. She has been struggling with the phobia of fear that came as a result of losing her husband.

If you have never gone through such an experience, you may find this hard to understand. But if a friend should share such feelings with you, don't be judgmental. Just listen to him and love him and you will help to heal him.

3. After shock and fear, often deep depression smothers one so completely that even a person who's normal will come to feel that he is losing his mind. Grief also makes us feel isolated and cut off from other people since family and friends who gave themselves so generously during the first days of grief soon get caught up again in the busy rounds of their own lives. Sometimes weeks, even months, go by before a desperate loneliness and grief overwhelm the bereaved person.

Depression is a normal emotional reaction to some cause, some disappointment, some fear that results in a feeling of hopelessness, self-pity, a desire to escape—and in extreme cases, even suicide. When depression comes, it is as though the lights of life have been turned out and we are left to wander in the darkness of despair and loneliness. We actually wonder if the sun will ever shine again and if we will ever laugh again.

4. Guilt is another natural response to death's wounds. In fact, guilt and grief often travel together. Sometimes it is guilt over a past illness—what we did or did not do. At other times it is guilt over all the "shoulds" of a lifetime.

All of us have hurt the person we have loved in one way or another. We have said sharp words, were sometimes inconsiderate and impatient, and acted selfishly.

In life there is another day, but in death there is finality. Death closes the door to making amends.

I have just left the home of a man who lost his seventy-nine-year-old wife. She had suffered a stroke and had been in the hospital for the past week. He had been with her day and night. The doctor had taken her out of intensive care the day before and she was apparently doing better, so he decided to go home and get some much-needed rest. Then about 3:00 A.M. she died.

When his granddaughter called me to tell me of the death she said, "He is on a real guilt trip because he wasn't with her when she died. He told me, "At least I could have been there to hold her hand and to say good-bye."

Feelings like this are not at all unusual. People often say to me, "Oh, if I had only done more for . . . " "If I had just called the doctor sooner . . . " "If I had been kinder to my . . . " and a thousand other things like that.

When death is by suicide the guilt is compounded. Not only do those who are left behind have to cope with the loss and the loneliness that ordinarily comes with death, but they must also struggle with embarrassment and terrible guilt. They wonder, "Shouldn't we have seen this coming? Should we have had him/her hospitalized?" Or, "Should we have stayed the night?"

A grieving friend may need to confess his guilt or regrets. If so, hear him patiently and nonjudgmentally. To listen lovingly is usually enough. A sense of guilt, like death, is universal. If it is real, then we might help our friend ask the Heavenly Father to forgive him and then to accept that forgiveness which is always available in and from God. If it is an imaginary guilt, then we might help him see that it is normal and well-nigh universal.

5. In grief, hostility also often rises to the surface. People become angry at life, death, God, doctors, and even the person who has died.

A few weeks ago I received a letter from a lady whose husband had died several years before. She wrote in response to an article I had written about Job in the *Baptist Standard*, our state denominational paper. She said, "Several years ago when my young husband died very suddenly I read Job over and over and I kept telling everyone I would never feel the things young widows are supposed to feel—the denial, the anger, etc. But later as the years passed I had to admit that I did have to work through every one of those phases—and the anger is still with me at times—especially directed at my husband for having an unannounced, unexpected heart attack and deserting me."

Not long ago a young man I knew committed suicide. When I visited with his family one of them told me, "I'm so angry at him for doing this to himself and to us. He was too young to die."

Can you understand such feelings? If you haven't been there, you probably can't. But if a friend should share such feelings with you, please don't be shocked or critical or feel compelled to try to explain why. Listen to him and love him; that is enough.

These five emotions almost always come with grief. So a person who experiences them is perfectly normal. We should expect them to come but we should not allow them to settle down and take up permanent residence in our lives. We must work through them or be crippled by them. The listening ear of a sympathetic friend can help us do that as much as anything, other than the Lord Himself.

So before I leave the matter of friendship let me remind you that "There is a Friend that sticketh closer than a brother" (Prov. 18:24). That's Jesus Christ Himself. As Jesus went to Mary and Martha when He learned of Lazarus' death, as He wept beside the grave of His departed friend, and as He wakened him from the dead—so Jesus will come to you, share your sorrow, and awaken new hope and new life in you. So don't forget to share your burdens, with the Lord as well as with a good friend. Both will help you to heal and become whole again.

chapter 8
TRUST—IN SPITE OF

A few months ago I received word that my mother had cancer in advanced stages. In over thirty years as a pastor I have heard that kind of distressing news about others hundreds of times. But it was different that day.

My mother must be the kindest, sweetest, most tenderhearted woman who ever lived. She would never knowingly say or do anything to hurt anybody. She is a remarkable woman.

Born seventy-five years ago in the piney woods of East Texas, she grew up milking cows, churning butter, drawing water from a well, cooking on a wood stove, and washing clothes in a washpot in the backyard.

She gave birth to four children and raised us through the hard years of the Great Depression. She never had expensive clothes, never learned to drive a car, never traveled more than 300 miles from where she was born, and never complained. Mama gave much and expected little in return.

Mother has a simple but profound faith in God that puts my faith to shame. As we talked that day about the future, she said two things that revealed her deep faith and her undaunted spirit. She said, "Well, your dad had cancer and Pat [my sister] had cancer, and I'm no better than they were."

Some people expect to be privileged characters in life, but not Mama. She knows that in a world of suffering and death none of us should expect immunity from anything. Nowadays when I hear hurting people ask, "Why me, God?" I want to respond, "Why *not* you?" What right do any of us have to think that we should not suffer, when even our Lord died on the old rugged cross at the age of thirty-three?

Then Mother said, "I don't know why this has happened to me, but I do know that God is not punishing me. I have lived for Him and He knows it."

Mother has what I call an "in spite of" kind of faith. In spite of the fact that my dad died with cancer, in spite of the fact that my sister died with cancer, in spite of the fact that she has cancer herself, and in spite of the fact that she does not understand why all of these things have happened to her, she is still trusting in God. It is this faith that sustains Mother.

It was the kind of faith that sustained Job also. When Job's troubles came, his wife suggested that he "curse God and die" (Job 2:9). Then his three friends came and tried to give Job intellectual answers as to why he was suffering.

They used the oldest and most common explanation for suffering known to man—the judgment of God. It was their opinion that if Job was suffering greatly he must have sinned greatly. So they kept urging him to confess his sins, to repent, and things would get better.

Job was not a perfect man and he knew it. He never claimed to be. But he also knew that his sins in no way matched his suffering. The punishment didn't fit the crime. So he maintained his innocence of any sins great and terrible enough to bring on such great and terrible suffering.

Though Job did not know why he was suffering so, he did know that his sin was not the reason, so he would not allow his wife or his friends to shake his confidence in God. He would keep trusting God "in spite of" what had happened to him. He expressed his unshakable faith in God when he said to his friends, "Though He slay me, yet will I trust in Him" (13:15).

Job's faith in God was not in vain. Before the Book of Job is finished God vindicates Job's confidence. In fact, the Book of Job closes with the statement, "So the Lord blessed the latter end of Job more than his beginning" (42:12). In the end Job's health was restored, his wealth was increased, and God gave him another family.

It is God's way to bring triumph out of tragedy for those who trust in Him. At least three times in the Bible we are told about people who exemplified Job's kind of trust in God. These examples have been placed there to encourage us in our days of adversity to keep trusting God no matter what.

Sooner or later we all experience troubles that we cannot understand and we feel are unjust. When those times come, we can either turn away from God in bitterness or despair, or we can keep trusting God "in spite of." One of the lessons of life that we learn from Job is that his kind of faith is the kind we all need during the adversities of life.

THOUGH ALL FAILS

The first of these examples is Habakkuk. Habakkuk may have been the first of Israel's religious skeptics. He saw the righteous being oppressed and the wicked prospering in his day and he dared to ask God why (Hab. 1).

One of the things that troubled Habakkuk most was that God seemed to be doing nothing. God appeared to be a silent and an inactive spectator to the injustices of life.

It is times like that, when God seems to do nothing, that are hardest on our faith. When Thomas Carlyle was well along in years, he became seriously ill and quite depressed. A friend was visiting with him one day and the subject of religion came up. The friend said, "I can only believe in a God who does something."

Carlyle reportedly winced as if in physical pain, and said with a sigh, "But that's the problem. He does nothing, nothing at all!"

This statement is by no means the full measure of Carlyle's faith. It simply represented the way he felt at that moment as the clouds of depression totally engulfed him. Yet I wonder, have you ever felt that way? Have there been times when it seemed to you that God did absolutely nothing, when He was, to use H.G. Wells' bitter phrase, "an ever-absent help in time of trouble"?

In Habakkuk's situation and in countless others the silence of God is difficult to understand. But we must remember that His silence is not due to inactivity or indifference. Far from being an unconcerned spectator, God is at work quietly, secretly, and imperceptibly implementing His designs, never too early, never too late, never in error.

Habakkuk's problem was that he simply could not see God working—and God felt no obligation to let him in on His plans. That is often the case with us. In the moments when we think that God is the farthest away, He is vitally involved in everything that is going on around us.

We must remember that just as it is possible to have movement without perception, God can be at work without our seeing it or feeling it. Let me illustrate. The earth is spinning on its axis at a speed of over 1,000 miles an hour at this very moment. Yet you and I have no sense of motion. At the same time it is rotating around the sun at a speed of 66,000 miles an hour. Do you feel anything? The earth is moving but we do not perceive it. Einstein used to strike two blows with his fist and then say, "Between those two strokes, we travel thirty miles." That's movement without perception.

Just so, God is moving in history. He is active in our world even though we don't see it or feel it. That's why we must not fling away our faith.

Finally the silence of heaven is broken and God speaks to Habakkuk. He tells His prophet that He will work a work in his day that he would not believe it even if he were told about it. Then, to prove a point, God lets Habakkuk in on His plan. He tells the prophet that He will use the Chaldeans as instruments of His judgment. They will sweep down from the north with the swiftness of leopards and with the fierceness of wolves and destroy Judah (1:6-11).

The Chaldeans were a cruel, barbaric people. They recognized no law but their own and worshiped no god but their weapons of war. This news didn't help Habakkuk at all. In fact, it raised more questions than it answered.

God was right; His prophet couldn't understand. God's ways are above our ways just as His thoughts are above our thoughts. So Habakkuk was left to struggle with the mystery of suffering and sorrow. But "in spite of" what was happening and though he did not understand, Habakkuk maintained his faith in God. He came to the end of his prophecy and gave us another one of the great expressions of absolute faith in God in all the Bible. Habakkuk said, "Although the fig tree shall not blossom, neither shall fruit be in the vines; the labor of the olive shall fail, and the fields shall yield no meat; the flock shall be cut off from the fold, and there shall be no herd in the stalls. Yet I will rejoice in the Lord, I will joy in the God of my salvation" (3:17-18).

It was Habakkuk's conviction that even if everything he had always counted on were to fail and there was nothing left—no figs, no grapes, no olives, no grain, no flocks, no cattle, nothing—he would keep on trusting in God and looking to Him for salvation.

There are times when we too must have a "though all fails"

kind of faith. Things happen to us or around us that we do not understand, and God does not explain. We should then keep on trusting in Him "in spite of."

BUT IF NOT

The second example of an "in spite of" kind of faith involves Shadrach, Meshach, and Abednego. Their story is probably familiar to you.

King Nebuchadnezzar of Babylon made an image of gold and then issued a decree that all of his subjects must bow down and worship the idol. Those who disobeyed his command would be cast into the fiery furnace. Shadrach, Meshach, and Abednego were young Jewish men who had been taken captive when Nebuchadnezzar conquered Jerusalem. They had been taught that it was wrong to have any God other than Jehovah and that they should not worship graven images. So they refused to obey the imperial decree and to bow to Nebuchadnezzar's golden idol.

When word of their disobedience came to Nebuchadnezzar, he was outraged. In anger he ordered them to be brought before him for investigation. He asked if the charges made against them were true. But before they could answer he threatened them and offered to give them another chance to prove their loyalty to him. If they would bow down before the golden image they would be spared. Otherwise, they would be cast into the fiery furnace that very hour.

To this challenge the three Hebrew children responded, "Our God whom we serve is able to deliver us from the burning fiery furnace and He will deliver us out of thine hand. . . . But if not, be it known unto thee, O king, that we will not" bow down before your golden image (Dan. 3:17-18).

Note the phrase "but if not." Our allegiance to God is not based on this or that answer to prayer. It is based on a confidence and a commitment to God that can stand the shock of unanswered prayer. For we know that if God doesn't answer a particular prayer, He is not doing so in order to answer a larger prayer, according to a larger plan and purpose.

Our commitment should be unreserved. Oftentimes in trouble we turn to God and when our prayers aren't answered we despair and give up. But our commitment must be deeper than that. It cannot depend on the answer to a specific prayer. That is not real commitment. We must keep believing when the prayer is not answered, and when our greatest fears are realized. That is real faith. Until we can say, "Though He slay me, yet will I trust in Him," we have not believed as completely as we ought.

You should pray that your loved one would be saved from his/her illness, and you should trust that he or she will be— "but if not" then you go straight on, unbroken in faith and confidence. You may pray that your son in war may be spared and brought back to you—and it is right to pray that prayer— but what if he is *not* spared? Then you will have to go steadily on, unbroken in your confidence in God. You will have to live on "but if not."

Our faith should not rest upon this, that, or the other thing happening, but on something unchanging—the character of God. That always remains.

You know the rest of the story. Nebuchadnezzar had the furnace heated seven times its normal heat and ordered the three Hebrew lads cast into it. The fire was so intense that the soldiers who cast them into the furnace died from the heat.

When Nebuchadnezzar looked into the furnace, he saw not only Shadrach, Meshach, and Abednego, but a fourth person who was like unto the Son of God. That fourth person may have been an angel or possibly a preincarnate appearance of Christ. We do not know for sure. But we do know that God was there, shielding His faithful servants.

Nebuchadnezzar ordered the three young men brought out and to the amazement of everyone they had suffered no effects from the furnace. Their skin was not burned, their clothes were not scorched, and their hair was not singed. There was not even the smell of fire on them. Nebuchadnezzar was so impressed that he praised the God of Shadrach, Meshach, and Abednego, and decreed that no one should speak evil of Him. Their faith was vindicated (Dan. 3:19-30).

There can be no natural explanation for such complete deliverance. It was their faith that brought deliverance, protection, reward, and glory to God.

We all need this "but if not" kind of faith of Shadrach, Meshach, and Abednego. It is the kind of faith that makes no demands of God. It keeps trusting Him "in spite of" what happens and though we do not understand why it is happening.

INTO THY HANDS

Jesus is the third example of the "in spite of" kind of faith we all need. Jesus' life was a life of faith. Daily He yielded Himself to the will of God as we should do. Obedience to God was never compulsory or automatic with Jesus.

His temptation experiences proved this. At the outset of His public ministry Satan tempted Jesus three times (Matt. 4:1-10). His intentions in these temptations were to lead Christ to sin and to thwart God's plan for man's redemption by disqualifying the Saviour. Had it been impossible for Jesus to yield to the temptation and disobey God, there would have been no real temptation.

Later Satan came to Jesus in a more subtle way. By this time it was clear that the cross was God's appointed way for world redemption and Jesus told His disciples that He must go to Jerusalem where He would be crucified. The cross was such a ghastly experience that it repulsed Peter and the other apostles.

So Peter, speaking for the whole group, tried to divert Jesus from going to Jerusalem. When he did, Jesus said, "Get thee behind Me, Satan; thou art an offense unto Me" (Matt. 16:23). Peter was sharply rebuked for aligning himself with Satan's plan to deter Jesus from fulfilling His mission. The harshness of the rebuke stems from Christ's fierce realism about His principle purpose for coming to earth, which was to die.

Though death by crucifixion was clearly God's appointed way, it was not easy for Jesus to go through with it. Until the very last He struggled with it. In the Garden of Gethsemane, He cried out, "O My Father, if it be possible, let this cup pass from Me; nevertheless, not as I will, but as Thou wilt" (Matt. 26:39).

The cup did not pass and Jesus died on the cross. In those last agonizing minutes of His life Jesus cried again, "My God, My God, why hast Thou forsaken Me?" (Matt. 27:46) In those dark hours of suffering and sorrow no one ever felt more forsaken, more desolate, more alone than Jesus did when He died on the cross. He cried out, "Why?" but no answer came. The voice of God that had spoken so often and so clearly at other times in His life was silent now. It was as if the heavens had turned to brass.

But, thank God, Jesus did not fling away faith. He had the "in spite of" kind of faith to say in His last dying breath, "Father, into Thy hands I commend My spirit" (Luke 23:46). Jesus unreservedly committed His life to God, certain that in the end God would not fail Him. And so may we. As you deposit your money in the bank in complete confidence, much more so may you trust your soul to God. The Creator of all things is faithful.

And in the end God vindicated Jesus' trust. He turned what appeared to be the greatest tragedy in history into the greatest triumph of all times. On the third day He raised Jesus to life, giving Him victory over death and the grave and completing our redemption.

But it would never have happened if Jesus had not said with Job, "Though He slay me, yet will I trust in Him" (Job 13:15).

James Stewart said, "It is when a man strikes rock bottom in his sense of nothingness that he suddenly finds he has struck the Rock of Ages." It was so with Job and it was so with Jesus and it can be so with you and me.

How often we look upon God as our last and feeblest resource. We go to Him because we have nowhere else to go. And then we learn that the storms of life have driven us, not upon the rocks, but upon "the Rock."

Following World War II someone found scribbled on the walls of a cellar in Germany this great expression of undaunted faith:

> *I believe in the sun,*
> *Even when it is not shining.*
> *I believe in love,*
> *Even when I don't feel it.*
> *I believe in God,*
> *Even when He is silent.*

Will you then say with Job, "Though He slay me, yet will I trust in Him"? Will you trust Him when all else fails, even if He doesn't deliver you from your affliction? Will you here and now commit yourself to Him unreservedly, even if you are left to suffer alone and in silence?

Will you say with me, and with the poet:

> As the marsh hen builds her nest on the
> watery sod
> So will I build my faith on God.

That was the way to victory over adversity for Job, and it is the way of victory for us also.

chapter 9
GETTING ACQUAINTED WITH YOURSELF

The Stoic philosopher Epictetus said that adversity introduces people to themselves. In times of trouble perhaps more than at any other times we do discover swiftly and painfully what kind of people we are and the quality of faith we have. Many people's Christianity is a fair-weather affair. A little rain and it runs and crumbles; a touch of strain and it snaps.

Without adversity a man can hardly know whether he is honest or not. A sailor cannot be sure of his skill until he has gone through the thick of a storm. A soldier cannot be sure of his courage until he has been in the heat of battle. An athlete can't be sure of his ability until he has undergone the pressure of the contest. And we cannot be sure of the quality of our faith until we have faced adversity.

People are like stained-glass windows; they sparkle and shine when the sun is out, but when the darkness sets in, their true beauty is revealed only if there is an inner light from within.

One of the lessons of life which we learn from Job is that when troubles come we discover what inner braces we have for the outer pressures of life. We realize for the first time what kinds of resources we have deposited in the bank of our spirits against the rainy days of life. Until then, we can't be sure.

At the outset of the Book of Job, Satan called the faith of Job into question by accusing him of serving God for mercenary reasons. The only reason Job served God, Satan said, was that God had been so good to him. With Job's wealth and health, a large and growing family, and an honorable reputation, who wouldn't serve God? But if there were some adversity in Job's life, it would reveal just how shallow and superficial his commitment was.

The Lord gave Satan permission to test Job in order to prove his faith. You know by now that Job passed that tough test. The way he endured his suffering and sorrow proved the sterling quality of his faith.

What can we do to develop a faith like Job's? What can fortify us against the day of adversity? What are some inner braces that can help us withstand the outer pressures of life?

In this life we are always between tears and laughter, meeting crises big and little. Just by being people, we are always in trouble—with hurt feelings, defeated ambitions, unrequited love, grief, or loneliness.

The real problem is not that troubles come, but that we don't have the resources to meet them. We run around feverishly to a lot of parties. We swallow tranquilizers and barbiturates; we lash out at people we care about; or, resolutely containing our grief, we come down with psychosomatic illnesses. Worst of all, we may find a refuge in bitterness, accusing other people, life, or God of tripping us up.

We need to know those things that will give us enduring strength for the stresses and strains that we must face in life. There are seven maxims I have found that we can add to our lives that will give us the inner strength to withstand the adversities of life.

1. ## LIVE ONE DAY AT A TIME

It has been my experience that those people who are best able to meet the stresses and strains of life are those who have learned to live one day at a time, cherishing the little things, the little happinesses when they come along.

"I believe that only one person in a thousand knows the trick of really living in the present," wrote novelist Storm Jameson. "Most of us spend fifty-nine minutes an hour living in the past—or in the future that we either long for or dread. The only way to live is by accepting each minute as an unrepeatable miracle—which is exactly what it is."

When we learn to cherish the little things of life we build up a reservoir of beautiful memories that will comfort and sustain us in the day of adversity.

Life can't all be like going to a fire or watching a parade. Most lives hold little that is dramatic and overwhelming. But every day has its quota of little happinesses—a cup of coffee with a friend; a quiet dinner with your mate; a brisk walk through the woods; reading a good book; or sitting by a warm fire. If we do not savor such little things, we may fail to taste life altogether.

The web of life is woven from threads like these. No thread alone is wide enough to encompass a sorrow. But, all together, they form a shelter that tempers the chill and slows the rain and softens sadness to the point where it can be endured. When recognized and cherished as they come, our small joys can build a reservoir of memories against sterile hours.

2. ## POSSESS A SIMPLE AND GROWING FAITH

Dr. Herbert Reynolds, president of Baylor University, recently suffered a severe heart attack followed by bypass surgery. At a dinner meeting preceding our next trustee meeting, Dr. Reynolds said to me, "I don't see how people go through an experience like this without the Lord." I replied, "They don't go through it as well." I have stood beside enough hospital beds and open caskets to know what I am talking about.

The next day in his report to the full board of trustees Dr. Reynolds said, "In times like these your theology becomes very simple. The things I found myself thinking about were the things I learned as a primary child—the little songs and the little verses—very basic and very simple. God becomes very real and precious in times like these."

I have found that the people who best handle adversities are those who have this simple, childlike faith in God.

But though our faith is simple and childlike, it should be growing. Faith is not a commodity like bricks. It is like a plant that grows. Faith is nurtured and sustained by prayer, by reading good books—especially the best of the good books, the Bible—by public worship, and by the meditation and solitude of private devotions.

We cannot rationalize away our sorrow and our loneliness, but we can make ourselves citadels of the Spirit against the storms of life. We must build up this resource in times of peace so that it will be waiting when it is needed.

3. ACCEPT LIFE AS HARD

Mittie Heavin learned last week that she has an inoperable malignancy that will require five weeks of radium treatments. She and her sister Annie Lee are both widows and have lived together for the past ten years.

When I visited with them in their home a few days later they talked in a matter-of-fact way about Mittie's illness and the prospects of her death. Annie Lee said, "We have always known that one of us would die first, leaving the other alone. And we have agreed that we will not grieve unduly. It will be hard and we will be lonely, but it is not right to let that ruin what life we have left."

It's people like Mittie and Annie Lee who accept life as difficult and are prepared to walk up to peril, grief, and disaster and do what is needed who best sustain grief and calamity.

Justice Brandeis once advised his impatient daughter, "My dear, if you would only recognize that life is hard, things would be so much easier for you."

Birth and death are bookends that go on each side of life and give meaning to it. The people who recognize and accept this are the ones who handle adversity best. Such strength, however, never springs to life the moment it is needed. It grows through the years, as we learn the discipline of meeting the little problems of life well and with courage in preparation for the day when the big ones will come.

4. KEEP SYMPATHY ALIVE

Another great resource is the resource of love. We are, in a deep sense, what our relationships to other beings make us.

Remember that the worst form of punishment that a person can suffer, short of death itself, is that of solitary confinement. There is a profound reason for this. Cut a person off from all contact with outside reality, and you have cut him off from the sources of vitality. What could be worse than that?

Abraham Lincoln said, ("To ease another's heartache is to forget your own.") And this is what Elizabeth Barrett Browning was getting at in those lines that state so well the Christian view:

> *A child's kiss set on by singing lips shall make thee glad;*
> *A poor man served by thee shall make thee rich;*
> *A sick man helped by thee shall make thee strong;*
> *Thou shalt be served thyself by every bit*
> *of service which thou renderest.*

If we keep sympathy for and understanding of others alive we will keep life from growing poor and brittle. Then in times of trouble the warm bonds we have established with other people will enable them to hearten and comfort us.

BUILDING CATHEDRALS

Work is yet another resource, as well as a great therapy. It soothes and relaxes the pain of adversity like few things I know. So, happy is the person who has a demanding work to occupy his mind. And the more difficult and challenging the thing we are working at, the better, for we can't work hard without using up some of the thinking that might go into self-pity.

And the more creative our attitude toward work, the greater enrichment we can draw from it. Do you remember the story about the three laborers that a passerby encountered on a Paris street working with great blocks of stone? "What are you doing?" asked the passerby.

"Cutting stone," said one.

"Earning fifty francs a day," said another.

"Building a cathedral," said the third. The people who are always building their cathedrals are mightily fortified against life's ills.

Austrian psychiatrist Victor Frankl spent years as a Jewish prisoner in a German concentration camp during World War II. There life, of course, was unbearably harsh and brutal. The prisoners were forced to work long hours and were given barely enough food and clothing and shelter to survive. As the months unfolded Frankl noted that some prisoners collapsed under the pressure and gave up and died, while others under the same conditions continued to cope and managed to stay alive. Using the tools of his psychiatric training, he could talk in the evenings to scores of his fellow inmates about this. He found a pattern beginning to emerge. Those prisoners who had something to live for, that is, an objective that gave a sense of meaning to their lives, were those who tended to mobilize their strength to survive. These objectives varied widely. One prisoner had a retarded child back home, and had a great desire to get back and take care of that child. Another expected to marry a girlfriend as soon as the war was over. Frankl himself had begun a book and had a fierce desire to survive and get it published. All these reasons made sense to the individuals themselves, meanings that welled up from within them and were not just superimposed from without. And they enabled these people to cope with the prison situation. On the other hand, those prisoners who had no sense of meaning soon "gave up" and either succumbed to disease or took their own lives.

Work is one of those things that gives meaning to our lives and thus becomes an energizing force that strengthens and sustains us against adversity.

MAINTAIN AN ATTITUDE OF GRATITUDE

To believe in the essential goodness of God and of life is another resource against the day of trouble. In 1970 I went to Africa for a month-long preaching mission. Most of our time was spent deep in the bush country of Uganda. The people there were among the poorest of any of the third-world countries. Their simple clothing had been patched and patched again. They wore no shoes and had no prospects of ever owning a pair. One day we were worshiping in a typical bush-country church. It had a dirt floor, mud walls, a thatched roof, and no furniture. Sitting on the dirt floor in front of me was a sea of black faces. We were singing the little chorus,

> God is so good,
> God is so good,
> God is so good, He's so good to me.

The Africans were singing in Swahili and I was singing in Texan. Right in the middle of the song the pastor-leader stopped, turned and pointed to me, and said with a smile on his face, "See, even our American brother can sing 'God is so good.' "

I thought, "My African brother, if you only knew how much we Americans have, you would know that of all people on the earth, we *ought* to be able to sing 'God is so good.' "

Then I realized that gratitude is more a matter of attitude than of resources. Thousands of people in America who have more materially than they could ever spend in two lifetimes have no song of gratitude in their hearts.

Those who have developed and maintained a belief in the essential goodness of God and of life have a strong inner brace for the outer pressures of adversity. To be sure, life is not always fair. But it is good and joyous, nonetheless. Believing that is a resource for life.

SEEING LIFE TO THE END

Finally, we need to believe in the ultimate triumph of righteousness. We cannot, of course, deny that tragedy is real, or dodge experiences, however hard they are to bear. But we can still believe in the triumph of goodness; we can maintain our conviction that we live in a universe where good is stronger than evil. Such an attitude is a shield against bitterness.

This is not always easy to do. To do so we must take the long look and see beyond the moment to the end of all things. Psalm 73 is the story of one man's struggle as he eventually comes to this realization. It is a leaf from his spiritual diary. Asaph tells us that he had been very badly shaken and that he very nearly fell. What was the cause of his trouble? Simply that he did not quite understand God's way with respect to people. He had become aware of a painful fact. Here he was living a godly life

and suffering all kinds of problems. He does not tell us exactly
what they were. They may have been illness, danger, trouble in
his family. Whatever they were, they were grievous and hurtful.
He was being tried and tried very sorely. In fact, everything
seemed to be going wrong and nothing seemed to be going right.

Now, that was bad enough in itself. But that was not the thing
that really troubled and distressed him. The real trouble was
that when he looked at the ungodly he saw a striking contrast.
They were prospering and increasing in riches. They were not
troubled like other men.

This almost threw him. It was not until he went into the
sanctuary of God that everything became clear to him. He was
put right and he began to climb up the ladder again, until
eventually he reached the top and could say that God is always
good.

When he came to the sanctuary of God, he began to see that
his real problem was not life but his own faulty and incomplete
thinking. He had not been thinking things through to the end.
The Bible says of Job, "You have heard of the endurance of
Job, and have seen the outcome of the Lord's dealings" (James
5:11, NASB). Job had been having a hard time, and he could not
understand what was the matter. He had not thought on to "the
outcome" of the Lord's intentions. The end to the story in the
last chapter of Job is that Job, who had been bereft of everything, ended up having much more than he had before. This is
the Lord's "outcome." Endure to the end in your thinking.
Don't stop short.

One trouble in life today is that people look only at the
beginning. Their view of life is what we may call a Hollywood
view. It is always attractive and all of those who live that life are
apparently having a marvelous time. Many people think that
life should always be supremely happy. But look at the ends of
some of those people.

The psalmist sees clearly that the whole position of the

ungodly is precarious and dangerous. They are "in slippery places." All they have is just temporary. And though at this moment all appearances may be to the contrary, it is as certain as the fact we are alive that the mills of God grind slowly, very slowly, and at times we think they are not moving at all—yet they grind exceeding small.

In conclusion, no matter what the state of the world, we should live in it with God-given courage. How well we do depends in considerable part on how well we have built up these seven timeless resources against the adversities of life.

If you haven't already, start today so that you will be ready when more rugged times come. Remember that you should not wait until the storm clouds are gathering to build a storm cellar. You do not wait until your house is on fire to take out insurance. You do not wait until thieves are prying open your windows to put in a burglar-alarm system. And you do not wait until the day of adversity to develop those inner strengths and resources necessary to stand against the stress and strain of life.

Start now living one day at a time.
Start now developing a simple and growing faith.
Start now accepting life as hard.
Start now keeping sympathy alive.
Start now building your cathedrals.
Start now having an attitude of gratitude.
And start now looking at life to its end.
Then when your day of adversity comes, you will be able to stand.

chapter 10
FREE AT LAST

The story of Job, as I said at the outset of this book, is a true story that reads like a fairy tale. Job was a prosperous businessman in the East. He enjoyed good health, a good reputation, a large and loving family, and he was deeply devoted to God. But through a series of tragic events initiated by Satan, he lost everything except his faith in God. His wealth was all stolen or destroyed by natural calamities. His children were all killed when a tornado hit the house in which they were staying. And physically he was reduced to little more than a vegetable because of loathsome boils that covered his entire body.

To make matters worse his cynical wife urged him to "curse God and die." Then his friends, reflecting the popular thought of their day, accused Job of some great sin; otherwise these misfortunes would never have come upon him. So Job not only had to endure his physical pain and deep sorrow, but he had to do it without the support of his wife and his best friends. In the course of these events Job went through just about every bad emotion that a person can experience and he had to draw upon every resource available just to survive.

Fortunately, Job's story has a happy ending. In time the Lord gave Job twice as much as he had before, restored his health and gave him a new family, and Job lived happily till he died at a ripe old age.

There is half a verse in the Book of Job that tells us when and how this all happened. The Scripture says, "And the Lord turned the captivity of Job, when he prayed for his friends" (Job 42:10).

Poor Job—what a captivity was his! He was captive to Satan, for the evil accuser had been permitted to test him by the malicious oppression of adversity, bereavement, and repulsive disease.

He was captive to his wife, whose complaints and bitter spirit vexed him day and night.

He was captive to the ironic verbosity of his intended comforters, who became unbending condemners.

And he was captive to the mental suffering of doubt, fears, depression, and despair.

But, good news! The Lord "turned" his captivity into an abounding reward which was far more than restitution. The exonerated patriarch was given more godly renown, more material wealth and domestic happiness than ever before.

Notice especially the agency through which his release came: "The Lord turned the captivity of Job when he prayed. . . . " Though it was the Lord Himself, and no other, who turned Job's captivity—as He is the One who turns all such captivities of His people—yet God made prayer the means. See here the indispensability of prayer in the affairs of life. Job's release did not come while he was argumentatively protesting his integrity against the cruel innuendoes and hostile bigotry of his friends. It did not come when he complained about his bitter experiences. It did not come when he questioned the justice of God, or when he persistently maintained his innocence. It was prayer which brought the miracle. Intercession was the invisible hinge on which the golden gate of deliverance swung open.

Prayer is always the gateway to getting help from God. It is the vital axis in the spiritual life of any Christian individual or church. Prayer, according to Vance Havner, is the only thing we can do that affects three worlds at once. It reaches up in worship to God. It reaches out in work to man. And it reaches down in warfare against Satan.

Most of all, however, observe the real factor in Job's praying which ended his captivity. "The Lord turned the captivity of Job when he prayed for *his friends*." This is immensely meaningful. It was not when Job prayed for himself that his liberation came, though that might have seemed the normal thing, but when he prayed for others! One of the high values of prayer is that when we earnestly pray for others, our intercession not only brings blessings to them, but it boomerangs back in blessings upon ourselves. Prayer for others has a liberating effect on us. If we spent more time in intercession, we would discover that our prayers for others were opening the gates of freedom from many a bondage in our own lives.

So we dare not neglect intercession, for it is the surest way to God's blessings on others and our own liberation. Psychologists agree that the best way to get tied up in a knotty bondage is to be continually thinking about oneself. Even prayer must be rescued from making circles around "self," or it soon becomes sterile.

What happened when Job prayed for his friends? God set him free from his physical affliction, from his emotional anguish, and from his mental anxiety. It was prayer that brought the miracle, the emancipation, the deliverance in Job's life, and it is prayer that can bring release in yours also.

What I want you to see in this chapter is that prayer is the most effective means of deliverance available to us from physical afflictions, from emotional anguish, and from mental anxiety. As prayer was the gateway to Job in getting help from God, so it should be the gateway for you and me. It was prayer that brought a miracle in Job's life and it is prayer that will most likely bring a miracle in yours.

FREE FROM PHYSICAL AFFLICTION

It was through prayer that Job was set free from the malicious oppression of adversity, bereavement, and a loathsome disease. When Job prayed for his friends, the Lord healed him of the horrible boils that had reduced him to little more than a vegetable. Prayer is oftentimes a means of such healing and deliverance in our lives and in the lives of others.

You may be asking, "Are you saying that you believe in miraculous healing? Divine healing? Faith healing?" Yes, emphatically so! I must admit that I am skeptical of professional faith healers, but not of faith healing. There are many miracles of healing mentioned in the New Testament. But there is nothing of the circus atmosphere that surrounds most "faith healers." And there is no record of the early church ever having highly publicized healing services.

I actually believe in divine healing more than most people. I believe that all healing, both the instantaneous and the gradual, is divine healing. A physician friend said to me recently, "Our job as doctors is just to keep people alive long enough for God to heal them." I believe that.

Moreover, I believe that healing should be a part of the ministry of every local church. The Apostle James wrote, "Is any sick among you? Let him call for the elders of the church; and let them pray over him, anointing him with oil in the name of the Lord; and the prayer of faith shall save the sick" (James 5:14-15). Prayer by the local congregation has always been a means of bringing the power of God to bear upon a person or a situation.

A word of caution is in order, however. This is not an

absolute and unqualified promise from God. If you believe that every prayer for healing will be answered, even all of those prayed in sincerity and in faith, you are destined to disillusionment. You will wind up like a young friend of mine whose father had cancer. When he received the distressing news, he immediately sought the best medical help available. In addition he began to pray and he called on his church and his Christian friends to pray for him also. But his father died, just as the doctors predicted. Sometime after his death, Steve said to his mother, "Mother, I think I've lost confidence in God. I prayed for Dad to get well but he died anyhow."

Everybody is going to die sooner or later. Death is an appointment we must all keep. As George Bernard Shaw once said, "Life's ultimate statistic is the same for all—one out of one dies." So the time will come when we will pray for the sick and they will die anyhow. James, who wrote the words, "And the prayer offered in faith will make the sick person well; the Lord will raise him up" (NIV), died. In spite of the fact that Christians must have been praying for him, he died.

Even Job, who was healed of his repulsive disease, died eventually. God sometimes chooses to work miracles in response to our prayers, and His Word commands us to pray for the sick. But there is no guarantee that God's healing will automatically come, and we must not be disillusioned when it doesn't.

The only way we can accept healing as an absolute and unqualified promise is if we look upon death as the ultimate healing for the Christian. Perhaps we need to see death in this light.

Richard Baxter was one of the great and godly theologians of all time. He was a preacher sent by God. The last years of his life were spent in physical agony. Despised, he spent many years in prison, hated and cursed by those around him because he was true to God in a time when piety was not popular. As he lay on his deathbed, a friend came to visit him. The friend pulled a chair up by the bed and said softly to the dying preacher, "Richard, how are you doing?"

And the great preacher turned to him and said, "Friend, I am almost well!" And he died. Think of that! "I'm almost well!" And he died.

There will be no blind eyes in heaven. No withered arms or legs in heaven. No pain or agony there. Tears will be gone. Death will be gone. Separation will be gone. This will be the ultimate healing. Then and only then, we will be free at last.

On occasion God does choose to act in response to our prayers and heal our afflictions. However, He does not give us any absolute and unqualified assurance that this will happen. We should pray for the sick, but we should not lose confidence in God if healing does not come. God may be preparing them for the ultimate healing. This one thing is sure—if deliverance does come, it is more likely to come through prayer than by any others means.

FREE FROM EMOTIONAL ANGUISH

The intensity of Job's suffering was increased by his emotional anguish. When his troubles came his dearest friends insisted, and even argued with him, that he must have done some terrible wrong to deserve what was happening to him. As a result of their insistent insinuations, Job felt betrayed, rejected, and falsely accused. The result was that he became bitter, angry, and resentful in his spirit.

These are destructive emotions that can master us. The sad and dangerous thing about hate is what it does to the one who holds it. Not only does it splash on those around us and corrode our relationships. It also, like an acid, eats away at our very souls. Anger produces physical changes in the body that are familiar to everyone. The heartbeat increases, the breath comes shorter, the muscles grow tense, digestion is affected, a person perspires, and he undergoes glandular changes that put him on the alert.

If we stay angry long enough, it can literally kill us. Fredrich Buechner in *Wishful Thinking: A Theological ABC*, writes, "Of the seven deadly sins, anger is possibly the most fun. To lick your wounds, to smack your lips over grievances long past, to roll over your tongue the prospect of bitter confrontations still to come, to savor to the last toothsome morsel—both the pain you are given and the pain you are giving back—in many ways it is a feast fit for a king. The chief drawback is that what you are wolfing down is yourself. The skeleton at the feast is you."

Anger, like any emotion, can be suppressed or repressed, or you may even deny it. But you can't fool your arteries or your blood pressure. As John Powell noted, "When I repress my emotions, my stomach keeps score."

You can't be free and happy if you harbor grudges, so put them away. Get rid of them. Collect coins, collect postage stamps, if you wish, but don't collect grudges, for they will destroy you.

The Apostle Paul warns, "Be ye angry and sin not; let not the sun go down upon your wrath; neither give place to the devil" (Eph. 4:26-27). You can't always keep from becoming angry. Anger is a natural response to provocation. However, you can keep anger from becoming a sin. You can handle it correctly. Anger should never be expressed in harmful or detrimental ways and it should be handled on a daily basis. Each new day will have a dark cloud over it if one enters it encumbered with the smelly garbage of yesterday's anger. Dealing with anger as soon as possible is the only way to keep it from growing and spreading like a poison throughout the entirety of one's life, developing into deep-seated resentment and bitterness. It is the only way to keep it from becoming a sin.

How then should we deal with anger? We should go to the

person we are angry with and be reconciled to him. Verbalizing our anger tactfully can produce stronger and deeper relationships. Second, we should forgive the person who has offended us. Anger is a choice as well as a habit. And so is forgiveness.

Finally, we should pray for those who hurt us. When we reach the point where we can pray for people who have hurt us, we are delivered from the emotional anguish of bitterness, anger, and resentment. We are free at last.

FREE FROM MENTAL ANXIETY

With all of the physical and emotional problems of Job came mental anxiety. He knew doubt, fear, despair, and depression.

In fact, Job gives us a classic picture of a depressed person when he says, "So am I made to possess months of vanity, and wearisome nights are appointed to me. When I lie down, I say, When shall I arise, and the night be gone? And I am full of tossings to and fro unto the dawning of the day. My flesh is clothed with worms and clods of dust; my skin is broken, and become loathsome. My days are swifter than a weaver's shuttle, and are spent without hope. O remember that my life is wind; mine eyes shall no more see good. The eye of him that hath seen me shall see me no more; Thine eyes are upon me, and I am not. As the cloud is consumed and vanisheth away, so he that goeth down to the grave shall come up no more. He shall return no more to his house, neither shall his place know him anymore. Therefore, I will not refrain my mouth; I will speak in the anguish of my spirit; I will complain in the bitterness of my soul" (Job 7:3-11).

Notice these ever-present symptoms of depression:

1. Apathy, lethargy, the blahs; life was empty for Job (v. 3).
2. Insomnia, erratic sleep behavior (vv. 3b-4).
3. Multiple physical ailments (v. 5).
4. Sadness, fear, worry, and a sense of hopelessness. He

sees no way out (v. 6-10). Most depressed people are overcome by a sense of helplessness. They feel trapped by the circumstances that brought on their depression.

5. Anguish of spirit and bitterness of soul (v. 11).

Dr. Bertrand Brown, director of the National Institute of Mental Health, said that depression is the number one problem in this country today. Depression is the common cold of psychological disorders. Almost everyone experiences it at some time.

Depression always results from a specific cause. The fact that the individual may not know the cause does not eliminate the fact that it exists. Depression is a result of our reaction or attitude to some problem or series of problems in our lives—a failure, a loss, a great disappointment, or rejection. It is not the event itself but rather our attitude toward it, our reaction to it, that produces depression.

Every state of depression includes a component of anger, at least in its initial stages. Whether visible or invisible, whether conscious or unconscious, anger is there. At first it is directed toward the person who has hurt, rejected, or insulted us. Later it turns inward at ourselves because of our part in the problem.

Then in time, anger moves to self-pity and utter hopelessness. Nothing produces depression faster or more deeply than self-pity. If the mental thinking pattern of self-pity is not arrested, the person becomes hopeless: the more he indulges himself in self-pitying thoughts, the deeper his depression becomes.

The depression formula then is this: some loss, disappointment, or hurt in life + anger x self-pity = depression.

I know something of what I am talking about. A dozen years ago I experienced a deep depression. It seemed as though the lights of life had gone out of me.

I had been working day and night, driving myself unmercifully as a pastor. In addition to the pressure of my work I was totally frustrated by the lack of cooperation from a fellow worker. I let the situation go on and on without dealing with it and eventually it ate a hole, called an ulcer, in the lining of my stomach.

This was a shattering blow to my ego. I had always thought that I was the kind of person who gave ulcers, not the kind who got them. This was an affront to my faith. Ulcers do not come from what we eat, but from what eats on us. Christians, especially pastors, I thought, should trust the Lord and not worry. My ulcer indicated to me a weak faith in the Lord. I was greatly disappointed in myself. I felt that I had failed God miserably.

Then I became angry. I was angry at the staff member for his lack of cooperation. I was angry at my deacons because they did not deal with the problem. And I was angry with myself for letting it all happen.

Then I moved to self-pity. I began to think, "I am thirty-eight years old and my ministry is over. Have I worked day and night for God only to come to this? It is not fair!"

I thought that I had worn myself out for God and now my life was over. I had a feeling of hopelessness. I thought I would never be well again. I was plunged into the depths of depression.

Can you see the pattern? A loss, failure, and disappointment, plus anger, times self-pity, equals hopelessness and despair. That's the way it works.

Ultimately the real culprit is one's mental attitude. If we aren't careful, we can be hijacked by our attitudes and then our moods can seize control of us. Our moods don't decree our thoughts. It is the other way around. Our thoughts govern our moods. Therefore, if you think right, you will feel right.

What is the cure for depression? First, we must learn to forgive people. Forgive those who sin against you. Depression-prone individuals are always conscious of a loved one or relative who rejected or injured them earlier in life. Until you forgive that person, you will never know lasting victory over depression. Someone has sagely remarked, "Forgive or perish." A human being is so constructed that if you prolong bitterness toward someone, it will ultimately destroy you. But if love replaces anger, depression cannot possibly intrude.

Second, we must not give way to self-pity. Self-pity is easily the most destructive of the nonpharmaceutical narcotics; it is addictive, it gives momentary pleasure, and it separates the victim from reality.

It's bad to sit around for a long time and feel sorry for yourself. Nothing separates us from others and from reality as quickly and as completely as self-pity. Don't let your feelings become the most important thing in your life. Don't brood resentfully about people and fail to respond to them.

The best way to stop feeling sorry for yourself is to start feeling sorry for someone else.

Somebody asked Dr. Karl Menninger, the noted psychiatrist, "Doctor, what should you do if you feel a nervous breakdown coming on?" Most of us would have thought that the great psychiatrist would have said, "See a psychiatrist." But he didn't. Instead he said, "Go to the front door, turn the key in the lock, go across the railroad tracks, and find somebody who needs you and do something for him."

So don't sit around engulfed in worry and self-pity. Get busy and help somebody else and you will be helping yourself.

Then pray for the person who has hurt you, as Job did. When you start praying for other people it means that you have gotten outside of yourself—you have overcome your anger and your self-pity. Then you will be set free at last.

So if you would be free, really free from mental anxiety, deal decisively with your anger and forgive those who hurt you. Stop feeling sorry for yourself. Get outside yourself and do something for somebody else. Pray for him. Then you will be free at last.

Poor Job! What a captivity was his! But what a deliverance God wrought. Job was free at last—free from physical affliction, free from emotional anguish, free from mental anxiety. Totally free, because the Lord delivered him. The Lord is the ultimate Source of our deliverance also. Seek Him through personal prayer and intercessory prayer and you may be free also. That's the only way to live, and to die.

chapter 11
HOW TO LIVE AND HOW TO DIE

Ernest Hemingway wrote that all true-to-life stories end in death, because life ends in death. At times, as we look around us, it may seem that evil is triumphant—but when you read God's love letter to the world, the Bible, you find that evil is always ultimately destroyed. It is true, as the Scripture says, that a person reaps whatever he sows (Gal. 6:7). Those people who sow good seeds will reap a good harvest. However, those who sow bad seeds will reap a bitter harvest. But it is important to remember that one's harvest is not always reaped in this life. If it seems that the good you do in Jesus' name goes unrewarded, rest assured that just as a sparrow cannot fall without God taking notice, neither can your good deeds go unnoticed. And if it seems that evil runs rampant and goes unpunished, be sure that the day will come when all unrepentant and unsaved doers of evil will reap the harvest which they have sown.

If you turn to the back of God's Book and read Revelation, you find that our side wins. In Revelation 12:7-11 we find these words:

And there was war in heaven. Michael and his angels fought against the dragon, and the dragon and his angels fought back. But he was not strong enough, and they lost their place in heaven. The great dragon was hurled down—that ancient serpent called the devil or Satan, who leads the whole world astray. He was hurled down to the earth, and his angels with him.

Then I heard a loud voice in heaven say: "Now have come the salvation and the power and the kingdom of our God, and the authority of His Christ. For the accuser of our brothers, who accuses them before our God day and night, has been hurled down. They overcame him by the blood of the Lamb and by the word of their testimony" (NIV).

We find that the saints (true believers) overcome Satan by two things: the blood of the Lamb—the saving work Jesus did for us on the cross—and the word of our testimony. By "word" of our testimony, the Scripture doesn't mean our eloquent speeches or sermons—but the testimonies of our lives as well as our lips. Want to defeat Satan? Trust in the Lord and praise Him with your lips and your life.

The time to begin a life of trust and praise isn't when trouble comes. The time to prepare is now. Or, if you're in the midst of storms while you're reading these words, begin where you are. Don't wait until a "better day" or until you're "in the mood." Begin where you are.

Look back again at the seven principles we discussed in Chapter 9 and make them your goals. Don't delay. When storm clouds gather, it is too late to plan a storm shelter. When you awaken to flames in your home, it is too late to arrange for that fire insurance you've been meaning to buy. The time to prepare for events is before the events come to pass. The time to build your spiritual foundation is now—because if you build on the rock of God's Word and His character and His Son Jesus Christ today, then you can stand in times of trouble.

It has always been ironic that many people who plan a two-week vacation in the greatest detail do not make any plan for traveling through life. In planning their vacation, they know exactly when they will arrive at their ultimate destination and just what they'll do when they get there. Yet they have not made any plan for getting to heaven.

TRUST IN THE LORD

If you want to know how to live and how to die, the first step is to trust in the Lord. The Bible says, "Trust in the Lord with all your heart and lean not on your own understanding" (Prov. 3:5, NIV). Job proves to us that we go far afield and get lost in turmoil when we trust our own understanding.

As the old song says, "I don't know what the future holds, but I know who holds the future." If you know the Author of tomorrow, then you can have absolute trust that, wherever you go, He will be with you.

Corrie ten Boom, author of *The Hiding Place*, tells how her family was put in a Nazi concentration camp after the Germans occupied Holland. Though her father and her sister died there, she took comfort in the words her father had given her in her youth: "There is no pit so deep that the love of God is not deeper still!"

David once wrote, "Where can I go from Your Spirit? Where can I flee from Your presence? If I go up to the heavens, You are there; if I make my bed in the depths, You are there. If I rise on the wings of the dawn, if I settle on the far side of the sea, even there Your hand will guide me, Your right hand will hold me fast.

"If I say, 'Surely the darkness will hide me and the light become night around me' . . . the night will shine like the day, for darkness is as light to You" (Ps. 139:7-12, NIV).

People have returned from places where evil reigned and pronounced them to be "God-forsaken places"—but the darkness reigns in such places because the people there have forsaken God. However, He is still to be found in the darkest night by those who want to find Him. He told Jeremiah, "You will seek Me and find Me when you search for Me with all your heart" (Jer. 29:13, NKJV).

Trust in the Lord and you'll know that He is with you throughout this life and beyond into the life to come. David, a man whom God said was "after My own heart," sums it up nicely: "Trust in the Lord, and do good" (Ps. 37:3). This is excellent advice for those of us seeking to know how to live and how to die.

THE LOSSES ARE REAL

Job teaches us much about suffering and how to react to it. His book also teaches us much about the causes of suffering. Job teaches us much about how to live and how to die.

The Book of Job ends much as it began. Once again, Job is prosperous; once again he has a loving family. Once again he is respected and honored. In fact, the Scriptures tell how God restored to him much more than Satan had taken from him.

God was surely, through all Job's dark days of disease and disaster and despair, working "all things . . . together" for his good. God does that for those who love Him.

The losses that Job encountered were real. After his trials ended his first children were still gone. And he still missed them. But for Job, as for all of us who are true believers, there was the certain knowledge that the children he had loved and lost were still waiting for him on the other side. Scriptures say, "No eye has seen, no ear has heard, no mind has conceived what God has prepared for those who love Him." True, they were on the other side of the veil and Job was on the earth. But just as he trusted God for his temporal life, so Job trusted Him for his eternal life.

When the child David sired out of wedlock lay near death, David fasted and prayed for seven days, spending his nights lying on the ground in anguish and agony. When the child died, his servants were afraid to tell him, because his grief had been so intense that they were afraid he would now do something desperate. But when David got the news, he got up, washed, put on lotions, changed his clothes, and went into the house of the Lord to worship. Then he went back to the palace and ordered dinner (2 Sam. 12:15-20).

His servants were amazed that he had grieved so intensely before and now was not grieving. When asked about this, David replied, "While the child was still alive, I fasted and wept. I thought, 'Who knows? The Lord may be gracious to me and let the child live.' But now that he is dead, why should I fast? Can I bring him back again? I will go to him, but he will not return to me" (2 Sam. 12:21-23, NIV).

David, like Job, knew how to live and how to die. While there is life, there is hope. And there is nothing wrong (and much right) in praying that God will intervene in our lives and bring us miracles. He is a God of miracles. But if He chooses not to, He is still a loving, gracious God. And we have the assurance of Jesus that "I go to prepare a place for you . . . that where I am, there you may be also" (John 14:2-3, NKJV). Our loved ones lost to the grave may not come to us—but we will go to them!

The struggle we are involved in is one of eternal life and death. We fight against a wicked adversary who is incarnate evil. Jesus has already defeated him at Calvary, and we are now in what soldiers call a "mopping-up action." But soldiers are still wounded and killed by the enemy even in the last skirmishes of a war. There will be times, in our battle, when

God will miraculously save. When it looks just as if the enemy will triumph over us, supernatural help comes. Cancers are healed. Crucial business deals go through. Marriages are restored. But when the miracles do not come, then we, like good soldiers, take our losses, certain that the Lord will ultimately restore all things to us.

There are few physical things more painful than some root canal jobs. If the nerve is dead when the dentist begins working on it, then it is relatively painless. But if you've ever gone in for one when the nerve was still functioning perfectly (perfectly *painfully*) then you're ready to come right up out of your seat when he begins. Yet, after a couple of days, the memory of that pain dims and, after a few weeks, you can barely remember it at all. After a few years, you can joke about it.

We live such a short time here on the earth. King David wrote that we are like grass—here today and gone tomorrow (Ps. 103:15-16). If we have received Christ as our Saviour, then we shall someday rule and reign with Him forever (Rev. 22:5). And just as an hour-long root canal seems pretty minor in a lifetime of 70 years or 25,567 days, so any suffering we undergo now will pale into insignificance from the standpoint of eternity.

John the Apostle was given a glimpse of that day:

And I heard a loud voice from the throne saying, "Now the dwelling of God is with men, and He will live with them. They will be His people and God Himself will be with them and be their God. He will wipe every tear from their eyes. There will be no more death or mourning or crying or pain, for the old order of things has passed away."

He who was seated on the throne said, "I am making everything new!" Then He said, "Write this down, for these words are trustworthy and true" (Rev. 21:3-5, NIV).

When a child of God really knows who he is and where he's going, Satan can never defeat him. Satan can torment, torture, and even kill him—but defeat him? Never!

How can we be defeated once we know whose we are? Once we understand that God is with us in times of trouble and we will be with Him in the times of triumph after Satan is at last cast down and we rule and reign with Christ in heaven, we are part of an unstoppable army. Jesus said the gates of hell will not prevail against His church (Matt. 16:18). We sometimes think of hell as being on the attack, but gates are defensive, not offensive. What the Lord was saying is that the gates of hell could not stop us.

When we come to understand that God is with us in times of trouble and that we will be with Him in times of triumph in eternity, then we know both how to live and how to die, and how to cope when the worst of things happen to the best of people.

chapter **12**
THE QUESTION OF THE AGES

The mystery of sorrow and suffering can so overwhelm us at times and so shake our faith in God that it causes us to question almost everything we once held sacred and true—including our belief in eternal life. This happened to Job and it can happen to us.

Job expresses his disillusionment when he asks, "If a man die, shall he live again?" (Job 14:14)

This question comes from the depth of his despair. As Job ponders the meaning of his own existence, he sinks into a sorrowful description of the wretchedness of life and the inevitability of death. He says, "Man that is born of a woman is of few days, and full of trouble" (14:1).

He sees his life as a flower of the field, cut from its stalk, soon to wither. He sees it as a shadow that will quickly vanish away. And he sees more hope for the stump of an old tree wasting away in a drought than he does for himself. All it needs is water for its old roots to sprout again. But death, Job feels, writes an inexorable "nevermore" on man's life. Once laid low by death, Job sees man as having no prospects of standing again. A tree has a chance for a second life after it is cut down. But with man, he figured, death is final.

As the finality of death occupies Job's thoughts, as the gloom of these pictures penetrates his spirit, he asks the question of the ages, "If a man die, shall he live again?"

This is really not so much a question as it is an expression of longing by Job. Moffatt translates his words like this: "If only man might die and live again, I could endure my weary post until relief arrived."

Job here compares his life to a sentry guard waiting at his post of duty through a long weary night. He endures his difficult assignment because he knows that the dawn is coming and he will be relieved from his post. It is the prospect of the dawn that keeps him going through the long night.

This longing expressed by Job is one of the deep longings of every human soul. Wherever man has been found, this longing has been found. The earliest traces of man discovered by anthropologists show that he has always had formal burial rites and even placed flowers in or on the graves of his loved ones. All of this indicates a belief in the afterlife. Man instinctively believes in a life beyond the grave. He believes it not because he can prove it; rather he tries to prove it because he cannot help but believe it.

From the beginning people have looked at nature and seen evidences of life after death. In the spring, green leaves appear on the trees. These leaves grow to maturity in the summer. Then with the coming of winter they die and fall to the ground. The dead leaves decay and replenish the soil. The next spring the whole process starts all over again. There is a sense then in which nature seems to say, "Nothing is ever lost; new life comes out of the old. Though all things die . . . all things live again."

And the findings of science confirm the appearances of nature. Science, for instance, tells us that nothing in nature, not even the tiniest particle of matter, can disappear without a trace. Nature does not know extinction. All it knows is transformation.

Now if God applies this fundamental principle to the most minute and insignificant part of His universe, doesn't it make sense to assume that He also applies it to human souls?

Logic adds still more weight to the argument for an afterlife. It takes a whole lifetime to build the character of a noble person. The adventures and discipline of youth, the struggles and failures and successes, the pain and pleasure of maturity, the loneliness and tranquility of age—these make up the fire through which he must pass to bring out the pure gold of his soul. It does not make sense that God would snuff out like the flame of a dime-store candle the existence of a soul thus perfected.

It seems to me that the character of God is at stake in this whole issue. He has placed in us a strong longing for immortality. It is a strange, restless feeling with which we are never quite at home on earth. Has God put that in our hearts just to mock us? Do you suppose that a good God would allow people to cherish such longings and then shatter them in jest? I think not.

It is from the depths of such longings that Job cries out, "If a man die, shall he live again?" These are the words of a man who cannot let go of his faith in a God whose present dealings are a blank mystery to him. Here is a man raising questions which the Lord alone can answer.

DUST AND DEITY

Perhaps I ought to pause and remind you that humans are the only creatures in the universe that could even ask such a question. The Greek word for man is *anthropos*. It means "the up-looking one." The rest of the animal kingdom looks down, but God made us to look up. People are a unique combination of dust and deity. Molding Adam from a lump of red clay, God "breathed into his nostrils the breath of life; and man became a living soul" (Gen. 2:7).

Thus people are different from all other creatures God has made:

Man is the only creature that has the power of imagination—the ability to dream, to think, to improve his life.

Man is the only creature that wars. Other animals fight individually, but only man organizes campaigns against his fellows.

Man is the only creature that clothes himself.

Man is the only creature that worships.

Man is the only creature that blushes—or needs to.

Man is the only creature that commits suicide.

Man is the only creature that both weeps and laughs. And why? Because he is the only one who knows the difference between the way things are and the way things ought to be.

Man is the only creature capable of being bored with his environment. All other living things are content just to exist, but man needs meaning in his life.

And man is the only creature who asks himself questions. He alone wants to know, "Who am I? Why am I here? Where am I going?" And he is not satisfied to live without answers.

So, the question of Job is really the question of every human. It is the question of the ages.

JOB'S QUESTION, JESUS' ANSWER

Job's question waited long for an answer. Weary centuries rolled away; but at least the doubting, almost despairing, cry from a man of sorrows of the Old Testament is answered by the Man of Sorrows of the New Testament.

The answer was in words given by Jesus, by the grave of Lazarus, to his weeping sister. In the presence of the great mystery of death He calmly, certainly, and confidently said, "I am the resurrection, and the life. He that believeth in Me, though he were dead, yet shall he live; and whosoever liveth and believeth in Me shall never die" (John 11:25-26).

Notice that Jesus, even in that hour of agony, turns Martha's thoughts to Himself. Who He is is the all-important thing for her to know. If she understands him, life and death will have no insoluble problems or any hopelessness for her.

He claims to have in Himself the fountain of life, in all possible senses of the word, as well as in the special sense relevant to that sad hour. Further, He tells Martha that by faith in Him any and all may possess that same life. Then He majestically goes on to declare that the life which He gives is immune from, and untouched by, death. His promise is that through faith in Him we can live until we die, and then we can go on living forever.

Physical death is not the termination of life. It touches only the surface life, and has nothing to do with our essential, personal being. For a believer to die is for him to live more fully, more triumphantly, more blessedly.

But these precious words, spoken to a weeping sister in a little Jewish village, which have brought hope to millions ever since, are nothing but words, unless Jesus confirms them by fact. If He did not rise from the dead, they are but another of the noble, exalted, and futile delusions of which the world has many. If Christ be not risen, His words of consolation are swelling words of emptiness; His whole claims are ended and the age-old question which Job asked is unanswered still, and will always remain unanswered.

But Christ's resurrection is a fact. "Now is Christ risen from the dead, and become the firstfruits of them that slept," wrote the Apostle Paul (1 Cor. 15:20). This fact, in connection with

His words while on earth, endorses them and establishes His claim to be the Saviour of the world. He gives us a demonstration of the continuity of life through and after death.

Along with Jesus' ascension, He declares that a glorified body and a heavenly home are awaiting all who, by faith, become partakers in Him. So, along with the saints of the ages, we can lift up our hearts in thanksgiving and triumphant challenge, "O death, where is thy sting? O grave, where is thy victory?" (1 Cor. 15:55)

So the question of the ages has an answer. And the answer that echoes from the chambers of an empty tomb is, "Yes! If a man dies, he *shall* live again!"

Since we shall live again, since there is life beyond, what effect should it have on us? What are the practical implications of our living after we die?

COURAGE TO KEEP GOING

The first is this: It helps make our present difficulties more bearable. It gives us the courage and strength to keep going in the hard times of life.

That's what Job said. If there were life after death, it would help him understand and explain his suffering. He could stand the torment in this life, if he knew there would be a better life to come.

This is the same truth that encouraged Paul to say, "For I reckon that the sufferings of this present time are not worthy to be compared with the glory which shall be revealed in us" (Rom. 8:18). "For we know that if our earthly house of this tabernacle were dissolved, we have a building of God, an house not made with hands, eternal in the heavens" (2 Cor. 5:1).

Hope, like nothing else, gives us the courage to hang on and to keep going.

Several years ago a doctrinal student in the Department of

Psychology at Duke University ran an experiment on this point with two identical rats. He put each one in a vat of water with only one differential. One of the vats was sealed shut while the other was left open. The vat that was sealed obviously had a limited amount of oxygen in it and no escape, and the creature that was swimming for its life in that context quickly perceived the static state of his situation. There was no apparent chance for him to modify things, and in exactly six minutes this creature instinctively gave up, sank to the bottom, and drowned.

However, the other rat, sensing that there was unlimited oxygen and a possibility of escape, swam for an incredible thirty-six hours before the experiment was mercifully ended. Now, whatever you may think about the morality of this use of animals, it at least highlighted the functional significance of hope.

We are all familiar with the cliché, "As long as there's life, there's hope." It is just as true that "As long as there's hope, there's life."

Hope of tomorrow, like nothing else I know, can keep us going in the dark and weary experiences of today. We are like the man who was taking his first trip across the Atlantic on a ship. He was so seasick that he thought he was going to die. A friend, trying to comfort him, said, "Don't worry, Friend; nobody has ever died from seasickness."

The sick man replied, "Don't tell me that. The hope of dying is the only thing that's keeping me alive." Without some sense of expectancy, life does break down and become unbearable. But with hope we find the courage to keep going.

ALL GLORY IS FADING
Second, the belief that we will live forever challenges us to live more nobly today. It causes us to rearrange our priorities in life,

to put first things first.

In Eugene O'Neill's little-known play *Lazarus Laughed* (N.Y.: Horace Liverlight, 1927), the brother of Mary and Martha comes back to the world with a strangely inverted sense of values. Maybe the "great" things are small and the "small" great. "Maybe we ourselves are greater than we think," he now believes.

Things do look different in the light of eternity.

There are a lot of people, especially businessmen, who are overcommitted to their work and undercommitted to God. They devote their lives to the accumulation of wealth, the wielding of power, and the building of a reputation, while they neglect the spiritual and eternal values of life.

Such behavior would be understandable if there were no life to come. But since there is, we must consider Jesus' question, "For what shall it profit a man, if he shall gain the whole world, and lose his own soul?" (Mark 8:36)

Jesus once told a story which answers that question for us. It was about a farmer whose land brought forth so bountifully that he had no place to store his crops. So he tore down his old barns and built new ones. When he was through he settled back in his easy chair and said to himself, "I have all I'll need for years to come. Now I can take it easy, eat, drink, and be happy."

But just when he thought he had it made, God said to him, "You fool, tonight you are going to die. Now who will get all the things you have accumulated?" (Luke 12:16-20) Isn't that the way it usually is? About the time we think we have it made, time runs out on us.

So Jesus draws this moral from the story: "Every man is a fool who gets rich on earth and neglects God." If there is no life hereafter then we too might just as well eat, drink, and be merry (1 Cor. 15:32). But since there is, we ought to seek first the kingdom of God and His righteousness (Matt. 6:33).

The movie "Patton" closes with General Patton describing

the final triumph of a Roman general as he returned home from a successful military campaign. The triumphant parade was led by trumpets and the strange animals from the country his army had conquered. Then followed chariots, laden with treasures. Before the conquering general marched the prisoners he had taken, in chains. And at last came the conquering general riding in his chariot. Sometimes his children, dressed in white robes, were by his side or riding on the trace horses. And beside him there stood a slave, whispering in his ear, "All glory is fading."

The Scriptures agree, "For all flesh is as grass, and all the glory of man as the flower of grass. The grass withereth, and the flower thereof falleth away" (1 Peter 1:24).

Unless our Lord returns first, we will someday die. We will have to face death, the enemy, and know death, and the new beginning. It cannot be prevented. But there is a great deal we can do to prepare for it. And one of the things we should do is keep our priorities in the right order.

Each time I think about my own death, I ask myself three kinds of questions to help me do that:

"Am I right in my relationship with God?"

"Am I right in my relationship with my family, with my friends, with my co-workers? Are there relationships I need to reconcile? Are there words I need to say?"

"Am I investing myself in things that will last for eternity?"

The more I look to the life to come, the more nobly it makes me want to live the life I now have.

BLESSED REDEEMER

The final challenge of the life to come is to cause us to put our faith and trust in the Saviour.

The despair that Job expresses in chapter 14 does not last forever. In time his faith triumphs. In chapter 19 he gives us the most momentous expression of faith found in the entire Old Testament. He says, "For I know that my Redeemer liveth, and that He shall stand at the latter day upon the earth; and though after my skin worms destroy this body, yet in my flesh shall I see God" (Job 19:25-26).

Job still regards death as imminent, for his wasted body is rapidly being destroyed by disease. But his earlier longings of a return from the grave to life again are now a firm hope. He expects the renewal of the whole man after death.

The word "Redeemer" is the Hebrew word *goel*. It refers to the next of kin or a close relative whose duty it was to take care of a man's property and good name after his death and, if he were unjustly slain, to avenge his death.

Throughout Job's whole ordeal of suffering and sorrow he has been falsely accused and slandered by his friends. Here he expresses assurance of a divine Redeemer, who will vindicate him in the last days. He is confident that the justice of God will ultimately prevail.

Job declares:

I know my Redeemer.
I know He lives.
I know I shall see Him and be with Him.

He knows this emphatically—without a doubt. This is one of the great confessions of all time. Job asserts his faith in God who will vindicate him even after his death. People may desert him. His family may fail him. But God never will.

And Job expects to be a spectator of his vindication from the vantage point of a body of flesh. Though his body wastes away, he will still be there in a body to see it.

Job doesn't understand how it can all be, but he is certain that if his body is buried and the worms destroy it, he will still remain alive; he will see God and he will be vindicated. Job knows that since God is just, there must be a reward beyond the grave. The nature of the reward is not thoroughly described until the New Testament. But it is enough for Job just to know that it will come and that he will receive it in person. Though Job still cannot understand the injustices he experiences in this life, he nevertheless clings to his faith in the God who has the last word, even after death.

We must not see Job as a modern Christian. But there is here the beginning of a progressive revelation that will lead to the second coming of Christ, the blessed Redeemer, at the end of time. It is a remarkable thrust of faith. Job in this passage catches just a glimpse of the glorious truth that comes to full light in the New Testament.

The revelation culminates in Jesus, who, according to Paul, "abolished death and hath brought life and immortality to light through the Gospel" (2 Tim. 1:10).

Through Jesus' death, burial, and resurrection, death has been conquered and our victory over the grave has been assured. Through faith in and commitment to Him, we can share in that glorious life.

We all know that death did something terrible to Christ, but not everyone knows that He did something wonderful to death. Jesus did not merely survive death. He conquered it. Through His life and death and resurrection, Jesus Christ defeated death. So the punch line of the New Testament is not a tragic cry, "Help"—but a triumphant shout, "Hallelujah!"

The resurrection of Jesus keeps the grave from being our final destiny. Eternal life is just beyond the door of death. Now, because of Him, we can live until we die, and then we can live forever.

Through the resurrection of Jesus, death has been translated from an ending into a beginning, from a period to a comma, from a conclusion to an introduction, from a final destination into a rest stop.

Jesus Christ, God's Son, died for our sins. He was buried in Joseph's tomb. He was raised from the dead on the third day and now lives forever. Because He lives, we can live also. But all who desire to share in that hope must come to Him in repentance and faith.

The poet John Richard Moreland expressed this truth beautifully when he wrote:

The hands of Christ seem very frail.
For they were broken by a nail.
But only they reach heaven at last
Whom these frail, broken hands hold fast.

We need to live and to die with faith in Him. He is God's answer to the question of the ages.